LIVING TRUSTS SIMPLIFIED

A STEP-BY-STEP GUIDE TO AVOIDING PROBATE, SAVING ON TAXES, AND KEEPING THE COURTS OUT OF YOUR FAMILY'S FUTURE

JAMES BROOKS

Legal Disclaimer

This book is for informational and educational purposes only and should not be considered legal, financial, or tax advice. The author and publisher are not attorneys, accountants, or financial advisors, and this book does not substitute professional guidance.

Laws regarding estate planning, probate, and taxation vary by state and jurisdiction and may change over time. While we strive to provide accurate and up-to-date information, we do not guarantee the completeness or applicability of any legal or financial concepts discussed in this book.

Before making any estate planning decisions, setting up a living trust, or modifying your financial plans, you should consult a qualified attorney, financial planner, or tax professional to ensure compliance with current laws.

The author and publisher assume no responsibility for errors, omissions, or outcomes resulting from the use or misuse of the information contained in this book. By reading this book, you acknowledge that the responsibility for any legal or financial decisions made rests solely with you.

This book does not create an attorney-client, accountant-client, or fiduciary relationship between the reader and the author or publisher.

Important Note: This book provides general information on estate planning and living trusts. Because estate and trust laws vary by state, you should consult with an estate planning attorney licensed in your state to ensure your documents comply with local legal requirements.

CONTENTS

INTRODUCTION

Making Sense of Living Trusts – Why They Matter

When people hear the term "living trust," they often assume it's something only the wealthy need—reserved for billionaires, celebrities, or those with sprawling estates. The truth is, a living trust is one of the most powerful and practical tools available for everyday people who want to protect their loved ones, avoid unnecessary legal complications, and ensure their assets are handled exactly as they intend.

If you have a home, a bank account, a retirement fund, or loved ones you care about, then a living trust might be one of the most important financial decisions you ever make.

What Is a Living Trust?

A living trust is a legal document that holds your assets—such as your home, savings, and investments—for your benefit while you're alive and for your heirs after you pass away. Unlike a will, which only takes effect after death and must go through probate, a living trust bypasses the court system, allowing for a faster, private, and more efficient transfer of your estate.

Think of a living trust like a safety deposit box:

- **You (the grantor)** create and control it during your lifetime.
- **You (or a trusted person)** manage the contents as the **trustee**.
- **Your beneficiaries** receive everything according to your wishes after you pass.

Unlike a will, a trust gives you more control, allowing you to specify when and how your assets are distributed—whether immediately, over time, or under specific conditions.

Why Do Living Trusts Matter?

1. Avoiding Probate: Keeping Your Family Out of Court

Probate is a court-supervised process that happens when someone dies with just a will (or without any estate plan at all). It's costly, time-consuming, and public. Your loved ones could face:

- **Delays** – Probate can take months or even years before assets are distributed.
- **Expenses** – Court fees and legal costs can eat into your estate, leaving less for your heirs.
- **Lack of Privacy** – Wills are public record, meaning anyone can see your assets and beneficiaries.

A living trust avoids probate entirely, ensuring your estate is settled quickly, privately, and efficiently—without the interference of courts or government processes.

2. Keeping Control of Your Assets, Even After Death

With a will, your beneficiaries inherit everything at once, which might not always be the best option. A living trust allows you to set specific terms for how and when your assets are distributed.

- **Want to ensure your kids don't get their inheritance all at once at age 18?** A trust lets you stagger payouts over time.
- **Want to make sure a family member doesn't squander their inheritance on bad decisions?** A trust can include spending restrictions and oversight.
- **Concerned about remarriage or protecting assets from creditors?** A trust can help shield your wealth from outside threats.

3. Protecting Yourself in Case of Incapacity

What happens if you become ill or mentally incapacitated? If you have only a will, your family may have to go to court to get permission to manage your assets, which is a slow, stressful, and expensive process.

A living trust ensures that a trusted person (your successor trustee) can step in and handle your affairs immediately—without courts, delays, or red tape.

4. Privacy & Asset Protection

Unlike a will, which becomes public record after death, a living trust remains private. No one (other than your beneficiaries and trustee) has to know the details of your estate.

Additionally, certain types of trusts can shield assets from creditors, lawsuits, or future divorces, providing long-term protection for your legacy.

5. It's Not Just for the Rich—It's for Anyone Who Wants to Plan Ahead

Many people assume that trusts are only for millionaires, but the reality is that a living trust can benefit nearly anyone with assets to pass down. In fact, if your estate is worth more than $50,000, a living trust may save your family time, money, and unnecessary legal battles.

If you:

- Own a home or real estate
- Have savings, investments, or retirement accounts
- Have minor children or dependents
- Want to control how your assets are distributed
- Want to avoid court involvement in your estate

Then a living trust could be the most important estate planning tool you can use.

What Happens If You Don't Have a Living Trust?

If you don't create a trust, your estate will be handled through probate, and if you don't even have a will, then the state will decide how your assets are distributed according to intestacy laws. This often means:

- **Your family has no say** – A judge determines who gets what.
- **Long delays** – Probate can take six months to several years.
- **Extra expenses** – Probate fees and legal costs can take a significant portion of your estate.

With a living trust, you take control of the future, reduce the burden on your loved ones, and ensure your wishes are carried out exactly as you intend.

Taking the First Step Toward Peace of Mind

Estate planning doesn't have to be complicated, expensive, or overwhelming. This book is designed to demystify the process, showing you step-by-step how to set up, fund, and manage a living trust that protects your family and your legacy.

In the next chapter, we'll start by breaking down the fundamentals of living trusts, so you can feel confident in making the right decisions for your future.

CHAPTER 1
LIVING TRUSTS 101

BREAKING DOWN THE BASICS – WHAT A LIVING TRUST IS (AND ISN'T)

A **living trust** is a legal document that allows individuals to place their assets into a trust during their lifetime and dictate how those assets will be managed and distributed after they pass away. Unlike a **will**, which only takes effect upon death and must go through probate, a living trust functions immediately and can be used to manage assets while the grantor is still alive.

A key advantage of a living trust is its ability to provide seamless financial continuity. If the grantor becomes incapacitated or unable to manage their affairs, a pre-designated successor trustee steps in to ensure that assets are handled according to the grantor's wishes without requiring court intervention. This is particularly beneficial in preventing the financial complications that can arise from guardianship or conservatorship proceedings.

TYPES OF LIVING TRUSTS

Revocable Living Trust

A **revocable living trust** allows the grantor to retain control over the trust while they are alive. They can modify, amend, or even revoke the trust at any time. This type of trust helps avoid probate and provides flexibility in managing assets. However, it does not offer significant asset protection from creditors.

This trust type is widely used by individuals who want to maintain direct oversight of their financial affairs while securing their assets for their heirs. It also enables the grantor to make changes in response to life events, such as marriage, divorce, or the birth of children or grandchildren.

Revocable trusts allow for the **appointment of successor trustees**, ensuring a smooth transition of management in the event of the grantor's incapacity. This prevents the need for court-supervised guardianship and allows for a more private and efficient handling of assets.

Irrevocable Living Trust

An **irrevocable living trust** cannot be altered once it has been created without the approval of the beneficiaries. While this type of trust offers enhanced protection against creditors and estate taxes, it also requires the grantor to relinquish control over the assets.

Despite its rigidity, an irrevocable trust provides advantages in asset protection, shielding property from lawsuits and reducing estate tax liability. It is often used for Medicaid planning and charitable giving strategies, ensuring that assets are preserved for designated beneficiaries rather than being exhausted by medical costs or taxation.

Additionally, irrevocable trusts can serve as a **strategic tool for tax-efficient wealth transfer**, helping high-net-worth individuals minimize estate taxes while ensuring that wealth is passed down through generations. These trusts can hold life insurance policies, business interests, and investment portfolios in a way that removes them from the taxable estate.

WHY TRUSTS ARE A POWERFUL ESTATE PLANNING TOOL

- **Avoids Probate:** A living trust allows assets to be passed on without going through probate, saving time and legal fees.

- **Maintains Privacy:** Unlike wills, which become public record, trusts remain private.

- **Protects Against Incapacity:** If the grantor becomes incapacitated, a successor trustee can manage assets without court intervention.

- **Provides Control Over Asset Distribution:** Trusts allow for structured inheritance, ensuring responsible financial management for beneficiaries.

Additionally, a trust allows for **contingency planning**, meaning the grantor can dictate specific conditions for distribution, such as setting age restrictions or requiring certain milestones to be met before an heir gains full access to their inheritance.

Trusts can also help individuals with **special needs beneficiaries**, ensuring that heirs who rely on government assistance continue to receive necessary financial support without disqualifying them from Medicaid or Social Security benefits.

WHY TRUSTS MATTER – AVOIDING PROBATE, PROTECTING ASSETS

The Probate Process – What It Is and Why It's Costly

Probate is the legal process through which a deceased person's assets are distributed. The court oversees this process, ensuring all debts are paid before beneficiaries receive their inheritance. However, probate can be:

- **Time-consuming** – Taking months or even years to complete.
- **Expensive** – Legal fees and court costs can deplete estate value.
- **Public** – Probate records are accessible to the public, exposing financial information.

A living trust circumvents probate, allowing beneficiaries to receive their inheritance **without delays, legal fees, or public scrutiny**.

The probate process can be particularly cumbersome for complex estates or when family disputes arise. A living trust eliminates many of the challenges of probate by ensuring **clear instructions** are provided for asset distribution, reducing the potential for conflicts.

How a Living Trust Helps Assets Transfer Smoothly

- **Immediate access** – Beneficiaries do not have to wait for court approval to receive their inheritance.
- **Avoids legal challenges** – Wills can be contested, while trusts are harder to challenge.
- **Simplifies estate administration** – Trustees can manage and distribute assets efficiently.

Furthermore, trusts are particularly beneficial for those with properties or assets in multiple states. Without a trust, an estate would have to go through **ancillary probate** in each state where assets are located, adding further delays and expenses.

PRIVACY BENEFITS – KEEPING YOUR ESTATE OUT OF PUBLIC RECORDS

A will becomes a public document once it enters probate, meaning anyone can access details about an estate. A living trust, however, remains private, protecting beneficiaries and keeping asset distribution confidential.

THE KEY PLAYERS – GRANTORS, TRUSTEES, AND BENEFICIARIES

Grantor

The **grantor** (or settlor) is the individual who creates the trust and transfers assets into it. They dictate the terms of how the assets should be managed and distributed.

Grantors often work closely with estate planning attorneys to draft a trust that reflects their long-term goals, ensuring that assets are preserved and passed down in a manner that aligns with their vision.

Trustee

The **trustee** is responsible for managing the trust according to the grantor's instructions. While the grantor is alive, they typically act as the trustee. After their death or incapacity, a **successor trustee** takes over.

Successor Trustee

A **successor trustee** is named in the trust document to step in and manage the trust in the event of the grantor's death or incapacity. Their responsibilities include:

- Paying outstanding debts and taxes.
- Managing and distributing assets per the trust's terms.
- Handling legal and financial obligations.

Choosing the right successor trustee is crucial, as they will be responsible for executing the grantor's wishes and ensuring the trust functions effectively. Many people appoint family members, but professional trustees, such as banks or trust companies, can also be designated to handle the role impartially.

Beneficiaries

The **beneficiaries** are those designated to receive assets from the trust. They can be family members, friends, charities, or any other entity named by the grantor.

Trusts allow for **customized inheritance planning**, meaning beneficiaries can receive assets over time rather than in a lump sum, reducing the likelihood of financial mismanagement.

Understanding Trustee Responsibilities

A trustee has **fiduciary duties**, meaning they must act in the best interest of the beneficiaries and in accordance with the trust's provisions. Their key responsibilities include:

- Managing investments and finances.
- Distributing assets fairly and according to the trust's terms.
- Keeping accurate records of all trust transactions.
- Ensuring all legal and tax obligations are met.

A well-chosen trustee plays a vital role in ensuring the longevity and efficiency of the trust, preserving wealth, and reducing the risk of estate disputes.

By understanding these key roles and responsibilities, individuals can make informed decisions when setting up their living trust, ensuring their estate is protected and efficiently managed for generations to come.

CHAPTER 2

MYTHS & MISUNDERSTANDINGS ABOUT LIVING TRUSTS

YOU DON'T NEED MILLIONS TO BENEFIT – TRUSTS AREN'T JUST FOR THE WEALTHY

One of the most common myths about living trusts is that they are only necessary for the ultra-wealthy. In reality, living trusts can benefit individuals and families of all financial backgrounds. A trust isn't about how much you have—it's about **protecting what you do have** and ensuring it is passed on efficiently.

Even if you have a modest estate, a living trust can help your heirs avoid the costly and time-consuming probate process. It ensures that your assets are distributed exactly as you intend, rather than being left to the state's default laws of succession. Whether you own a home, have savings, or simply want to avoid unnecessary legal complications, a living trust can provide peace of mind.

Additionally, a trust allows you to set conditions on inheritance, which can be particularly beneficial if you have minor children or heirs who may not be financially responsible. By establishing a trust, you can ensure that assets are distributed over time rather than in a single lump sum, preventing potential financial mismanagement. Trusts can also be structured to provide for beneficiaries with special needs, ensuring they receive financial support without jeopardizing their eligibility for government assistance.

Another important aspect of living trusts is their ability to protect assets from creditors and legal disputes. While revocable trusts do not offer strong asset protection, an irrevocable trust can shield wealth from lawsuits, divorces, and other financial threats. This is especially useful for individuals in high-risk professions or those with concerns about future liability.

Furthermore, living trusts provide flexibility for long-term financial planning. Trusts can be structured to hold and manage assets over generations, ensuring that your wealth is preserved and distributed according to your long-term vision. By utilizing different types of trusts, such as dynasty trusts, families can establish long-lasting financial security that spans multiple generations.

THE COST FACTOR – WHY A LIVING TRUST MIGHT SAVE YOU MORE THAN IT COSTS

Another common misconception is that setting up a living trust is prohibitively expensive. While creating a trust does involve an upfront legal cost, it is often **far less expensive than the costs associated with probate**.

The True Costs of Probate vs. a Living Trust

- **Probate fees**: Court costs, attorney fees, and administrative expenses can consume anywhere from **3% to 7%** of an estate's total value. For a $300,000 estate, that could mean $9,000 to $21,000 in unnecessary fees.

• **Time delays**: Probate can take months—or even years—to finalize, causing financial hardship for your heirs. A trust, on the other hand, allows for immediate asset distribution.

• **Privacy concerns**: Probate is a public process, meaning anyone can access your estate records. A living trust keeps your financial affairs confidential.

A well-drafted living trust may require an initial legal investment, but compared to the **potential costs and delays of probate**, it is a financial decision that often **saves families thousands of dollars in the long run**. Additionally, the peace of mind that comes with knowing your loved ones won't have to deal with unnecessary legal hurdles is priceless.

Another overlooked benefit is that a living trust simplifies multi-state asset management. If you own real estate in multiple states, your estate could be subject to multiple probate proceedings. A trust eliminates the need for this, ensuring a smoother transition of assets. This can be particularly valuable for individuals who own vacation homes or rental properties in different jurisdictions.

Additionally, having a trust in place can significantly reduce the chances of legal disputes among beneficiaries. Wills are often contested in court, leading to prolonged legal battles, whereas trusts provide clearer directives and less opportunity for challenges. This makes living trusts a valuable tool in ensuring that your wishes are carried out smoothly and without conflict.

IRREVOCABLE VS. REVOCABLE TRUSTS – KNOWING THE DIFFERENCE

Another area of confusion is the difference between **revocable and irrevocable** trusts. Many people assume that all trusts operate the same way, leading to misconceptions about flexibility and control.

Revocable Trusts

• Allow the grantor to **retain full control** over assets during their lifetime.

• Can be modified, changed, or even revoked at any time.

• Help avoid probate but do not provide asset protection from creditors.

Revocable trusts are the most common type of living trust because they allow the grantor to remain in full control of their assets while enjoying the benefits of probate avoidance. These trusts are ideal for individuals who want flexibility in their estate planning while ensuring a smooth transfer of assets to their beneficiaries. However, one misconception about revocable trusts is that they protect assets from lawsuits or nursing home costs. Since the grantor retains control, assets in a revocable trust are still considered part of their estate for legal and tax purposes.

Irrevocable Trusts

• Once established, **cannot be altered without beneficiary consent**.

• Provide **strong asset protection**, shielding wealth from lawsuits and estate taxes.

• Are often used for Medicaid planning or charitable giving.

An irrevocable trust, on the other hand, provides significant asset protection but at the cost of flexibility. Once assets are transferred into an irrevocable trust, the grantor gives up ownership, meaning creditors and lawsuits generally cannot access these funds. This type of trust is often used for Medicaid planning, allowing individuals to qualify for government assistance while preserving their wealth for their heirs.

A common myth about irrevocable trusts is that they are only for people with extensive wealth. However, individuals of all income levels can benefit from this type of trust, particularly those who are planning for long-term care expenses or have concerns about protecting assets from potential future legal actions.

Another key advantage of irrevocable trusts is their ability to provide tax benefits. By removing assets from the grantor's estate, irrevocable trusts can reduce estate tax liability, making them a useful tool for high-net-worth individuals looking to minimize taxes. Additionally, they can serve as a strategic method for charitable giving, ensuring that assets benefit chosen charities while providing tax deductions for the grantor.

WHAT DOES A LIVING TRUST ACTUALLY COST?

One of the most common questions people ask is, "How much does it cost to set up a living trust?" The answer depends on the complexity of your estate, your location, and whether you choose to work with an attorney or use a DIY solution. Below are general cost estimates to help set expectations:

Attorney-Drafted Living Trust

- **Simple Revocable Living Trust:** $1,000 – $3,000

◦ Suitable for individuals or couples with straightforward estates

- **Complex Trusts or Blended Family Planning:** $3,000 – $6,000+

◦ Includes additional provisions for second marriages, minor children, asset protection, or special needs

• **High-Net-Worth or Tax-Driven Plans:** $5,000 – $15,000+

◦ May include irrevocable trusts, tax sheltering strategies, business interests, and charitable giving tools

DIY and Online Trust Services

• **Online or Software-Based Trust Kits:** $100 – $500

◦ Typically includes fill-in-the-blank templates and basic instructions

◦ Best suited for very simple estates and individuals comfortable with legal forms

◦ *Caution:* These often lack proper customization and legal review, which can lead to costly issues later

Ongoing Costs

• **Amendments or Updates:** $200 – $1,000 (if done through an attorney)

• **Trust Reviews (every 3–5 years):** Often $300 – $750

Professional Trustee Fees (if applicable)

• **Bank or Corporate Trustee Services:** 0.5% – 1.5% of trust assets annually

◦ Some have minimum fees (e.g., $2,500/year)

◦ Ideal for large or complex estates, or when a neutral third party is preferred

Additional Costs to Consider

• **Deed Transfers (real estate into trust):** $150 – $500 per property (plus county recording fees)

• **Asset Titling Assistance:** Some attorneys include this in their package; others charge hourly

- **Notarization and Witnessing Fees:** Usually minimal, but may apply depending on your state

These figures are only rough estimates and can vary widely. The key takeaway: a well-crafted trust is an investment in protecting your estate and avoiding far greater costs later—such as probate fees, legal disputes, and tax inefficiencies.

CONCLUSION

Understanding these myths and misconceptions is crucial to making an informed estate planning decision. Living trusts are **not just for the wealthy**, they are **not prohibitively expensive**, and they provide significant benefits in terms of **control, privacy, and financial security**. By debunking these common misunderstandings, individuals can take the necessary steps to **protect their assets and their loved ones** for the future.

A well-structured living trust can serve as a vital component of any estate plan, offering benefits that extend far beyond avoiding probate. Whether ensuring smooth asset distribution, protecting beneficiaries, or securing financial privacy, a trust is a powerful tool that can adapt to the needs of virtually anyone. If you're considering setting up a trust, consulting with an estate planning professional can help tailor a plan that best meets your unique situation.

By taking action today, you can secure a **future free from legal uncertainty and financial complications**, giving both yourself and your loved ones peace of mind.

CHAPTER 3

THE TRUE BENEFITS OF A LIVING TRUST

SKIPPING PROBATE – KEEPING YOUR FAMILY OUT OF COURT

One of the most significant advantages of a living trust is that it allows your estate to bypass **probate**, the court-supervised process of distributing assets after death. Probate can be time-consuming, costly, and emotionally draining for your loved ones. Without a trust, probate may lead to legal disputes, delays, and unnecessary expenses that could reduce the value of your estate.

THE DOWNSIDES OF PROBATE

• **Lengthy delays** – Probate can take **months or even years,** leaving heirs waiting for their inheritance, particularly if legal challenges arise.

• **Expensive legal fees** – Attorney costs, court fees, and administrative expenses can quickly add up, often consuming a significant portion of the estate.

- **Lack of privacy** – Probate records are public, meaning anyone can access details about your assets and beneficiaries. This can expose sensitive financial information to outsiders.
- **Court intervention** – A judge ultimately oversees probate, which can result in decisions that do not align with the deceased's intentions.

A living trust **completely avoids probate**, ensuring that your heirs receive their inheritance quickly and efficiently. Because a trustee manages the distribution process privately, there is no need for court intervention, reducing stress and costs for your family.

IMMEDIATE ACCESS TO ASSETS

When an individual passes away with only a will (or no estate plan at all), their assets can be **frozen** during the probate process. This can create financial strain for surviving family members who may need immediate access to funds. A living trust allows assets to be distributed **immediately or according to a predetermined schedule**, ensuring that beneficiaries can cover funeral costs, mortgage payments, and daily expenses without delays.

Additionally, a living trust ensures that assets do not get tied up in unnecessary legal battles or disputes among heirs. By clearly outlining distribution plans, a trust **reduces the likelihood of family conflicts** and prevents courts from making decisions that may not align with your wishes.

A well-structured trust can also help protect assets from **creditors or lawsuits**, ensuring that your estate remains intact for your beneficiaries. In cases of blended families, where multiple children from different relationships are involved, a trust can provide **equitable distribution** and prevent disputes among heirs.

YOUR LEGACY, YOUR RULES – SETTING CONDITIONS FOR INHERITANCE

A major benefit of a living trust is the ability to dictate exactly **how and when** assets are distributed to beneficiaries. Unlike a will, which typically provides an outright lump sum inheritance, a trust can set conditions and **protect heirs from financial mismanagement**.

CUSTOMIZABLE INHERITANCE TERMS

With a trust, you can:

- **Delay inheritance** – Instead of an 18-year-old receiving a large sum all at once, funds can be distributed gradually (e.g., 25% at age 25, 50% at age 30, and the remainder at age 35).
- **Protect vulnerable heirs** – If a beneficiary has a history of financial irresponsibility, you can ensure their inheritance is managed responsibly through a trustee, preventing reckless spending.
- **Provide for special needs beneficiaries** – A **special needs trust** allows heirs with disabilities to receive financial support **without jeopardizing government benefits** like Medicaid or Supplemental Security Income (SSI).
- **Encourage education and career growth** – Funds can be released upon graduation from college, obtaining a professional degree, or reaching other personal milestones, ensuring responsible financial decisions.

- **Ensure long-term financial stability** – Trusts can be structured to provide consistent financial support over decades, ensuring that beneficiaries have access to funds throughout their lifetime while preventing financial mismanagement.

- **Restrict reckless spending** – You can structure distributions over time or appoint a financial advisor as trustee to provide oversight.

- **Set charitable contributions** – If you wish to donate a portion of your estate to charity, a trust allows you to structure planned giving while maintaining control over how funds are used.

By structuring distributions, you can prevent poor financial decisions and provide long-term stability for your loved ones. This added control is especially useful in complex family situations, such as blended families or estranged relatives, where an outright inheritance might not align with the grantor's intentions.

PROTECTING VULNERABLE BENEFICIARIES – SAFEGUARDING MINORS & SPECIAL NEEDS HEIRS

A living trust can be especially beneficial for **minor children** and heirs with **special needs**. Courts do not allow minors to inherit assets directly, which means their inheritance would be managed by a court-appointed guardian until they reach legal adulthood. This can lead to **costly and impersonal oversight** that may not align with your wishes.

MINORS & GUARDIANSHIP ISSUES

- Without a trust, a judge decides who manages a child's

inheritance, which may not be the person you would have chosen.

- Court-appointed guardianship can be **costly, bureaucratic, and restrictive**, leading to delayed access to essential funds.

- Once a child turns 18, they may receive a **large, unrestricted lump sum** with no safeguards, making them susceptible to poor financial decisions.

- A trust allows you to appoint **a trusted individual** to manage funds until the child is financially responsible, reducing the risk of squandered inheritance.

- Funds can be directed for specific purposes like **education, healthcare, or housing** to ensure responsible usage.

By setting up a trust, you ensure that funds are used for a child's **education, healthcare, and basic needs**, rather than being spent unwisely. Many parents use trusts to distribute funds gradually, preventing young adults from making poor financial decisions early in life.

SPECIAL NEEDS PLANNING

Heirs with disabilities may rely on government assistance programs like Medicaid or Supplemental Security Income (SSI). A direct inheritance could disqualify them from these benefits. By setting up a **Special Needs Trust (SNT)**, you can:

- Provide **financial support** without disqualifying the heir from assistance programs.

- Ensure funds are used for medical expenses, education, and quality-of-life improvements.

- Appoint a trustee to manage the trust in the beneficiary's best interest, ensuring financial oversight.

• Guarantee **lifelong financial security**, ensuring the individual is cared for well into the future.

• Protect funds from creditors or misuse, ensuring that the inheritance is used for necessary expenses.

• Structure distributions in a way that supplements but does not replace government assistance, maintaining eligibility for disability benefits.

By incorporating these safeguards, you ensure that your most vulnerable loved ones are protected and supported. This type of planning helps provide peace of mind to parents and family members who worry about what will happen when they are no longer there to provide for a special needs individual.

CONCLUSION

A living trust offers **far more than just avoiding probate**—it provides customized, flexible solutions that give you complete control over how your assets are handled after your passing. Whether you're looking to **simplify the inheritance process, protect your loved ones, or prevent financial mismanagement**, a living trust is one of the most effective tools in estate planning.

A trust ensures that **estate distribution happens seamlessly, privately, and according to your exact wishes**. Unlike a will, which becomes public record, a trust allows your beneficiaries to inherit **without outside interference**.

By establishing a trust now, you can **secure your legacy, protect your family, and create financial stability for future generations**. Taking proactive steps today ensures that your estate is handled on your terms, offering peace of mind for both you and your heirs. Trust planning isn't just about distributing assets—it's about preserving your values, ensuring long-term financial security, and protecting those who matter most.

CASE STUDY: AVOIDING PROBATE WITH A LIVING TRUST

When Susan passed away at age 74, her family was prepared. Years earlier, she had created a revocable living trust and carefully transferred her home, savings, and investment accounts into it. She had also named her oldest daughter, Kim, as successor trustee.

After Susan's death, Kim was able to immediately begin managing the trust. With a copy of the trust document and her mother's death certificate, she contacted the banks, retitled the accounts, and began distributing assets to her siblings according to the instructions in the trust.

Because everything had been properly transferred into the trust, Susan's estate completely avoided probate. There were no court hearings, no delays, and no costly attorney fees. The entire process took less than two months. Her children received their inheritances privately and without added stress during a difficult time.

This case highlights how proactive trust planning can save families time, money, and unnecessary legal complications.

CHAPTER 4

CREATING YOUR LIVING TRUST

DESIGNING YOUR ESTATE PLAN – A STEP-BY-STEP GUIDE

Creating a living trust is one of the most effective ways to secure your assets and provide for your loved ones. While it may seem complex, breaking the process down into clear, manageable steps makes it much easier to accomplish. A well-structured trust ensures that your wishes are carried out precisely as intended, avoiding costly legal complications for your heirs and ensuring a seamless transition of wealth.

⚠ *Trust laws, property titling, and deed recording requirements can vary by state. When in doubt, consult a local estate planning attorney to avoid delays or probate issues later.*

STEP 1: IDENTIFY YOUR GOALS AND NEEDS

Before drafting your trust, consider what you want to achieve. Ask yourself:

• Who will be your beneficiaries, and how should assets be distributed among them?

• Do you want to place conditions on inheritance, such as age restrictions or educational requirements?

• Who will serve as your trustee, and who will step in as a successor trustee if needed?

• Do you have minor children or dependents who require special provisions, such as a guardian or a special needs trust?

• Are there charitable organizations or causes you wish to support through your trust?

• Will you need asset protection measures to safeguard against creditors or lawsuits?

Defining these objectives will help tailor your living trust to meet your unique needs, ensuring that all financial, personal, and legal considerations are addressed in advance. A well-thought-out trust ensures that your legacy is protected and distributed according to your exact intentions.

STEP 2: CHOOSE THE RIGHT TYPE OF TRUST

There are different types of living trusts, and choosing the right one depends on your estate planning goals. Each type has its own advantages, depending on your financial situation and long-term planning needs.

• **Revocable Living Trust:** Offers flexibility, allowing you to make changes as long as you are alive. Ideal for individuals who wish to retain control over their assets while alive. This type of trust helps avoid probate but does not offer asset protection from creditors or lawsuits.

• **Irrevocable Living Trust:** Provides asset protection and tax benefits but cannot be changed easily once created. Typically used for Medicaid planning, wealth preservation, and reducing estate tax burdens.

• **Specialized Trusts:** These may include special needs trusts for dependents, charitable trusts for philanthropic giving, or dynasty trusts to pass wealth through generations.

• **Spendthrift Trusts:** Designed for beneficiaries who may not be financially responsible, protecting assets from creditors, poor financial decisions, or divorce settlements.

• **Asset Protection Trusts:** Used to safeguard assets from lawsuits, creditors, or financial mismanagement while still allowing beneficiaries to receive distributions under defined terms.

Quick Guide to Common Trust Types

Trust Type	Revocable?	Asset Protection?	Avoids Probate?	Best Used For
Revocable Living Trust	Yes	✓	✓	General estate planning: retaining control while alive
Irrevocable Trust	No	✓	✓	Medicaid planning, tax reduction, creditor protection
Special Needs Trust (SNT)	No	✓	✓	Supporting disabled heir without affecting public benefits
Charitable Remainder Trust	No	✓	✓	Providing income during life, with remainder going to charty
Asset Protection Trust	No	✓	✓	Shielding asets from lawsuits, divorce, or creditors
Qualified Personal Residence Trust (QPRT)	No	✓	✓	Transferring a home whie reducing estate tax value
Dynasty Trust Annuity Trust (GRA)	No	✓	✓	Passesing wealth across multiple annuity payments

STEP 3: LIST AND ORGANIZE YOUR ASSETS

Taking an inventory of your assets ensures that everything is accounted for when funding your trust. This includes:

- **Real estate properties** – Primary residences, vacation homes, rental properties, and undeveloped land.
- **Bank accounts and investment portfolios** – Checking, savings, brokerage accounts, and stock holdings.
- **Retirement accounts and life insurance policies** – Ensuring proper beneficiary designations for tax efficiency.
- **Business interests and intellectual property** – Ensuring that business succession plans align with your trust.
- **Valuable personal property** – Art, jewelry, vehicles, collectibles, antiques, and heirlooms.
- **Digital assets** – Cryptocurrency, domain names, online accounts, intellectual property, and monetized online content.

A detailed asset inventory will make it easier to ensure that all assets are properly transferred into the trust, preventing potential probate issues or inheritance disputes.

STEP 4: CHOOSE A TRUSTEE

A trustee is responsible for managing the trust and distributing assets according to your instructions. Selecting the right trustee is crucial to ensuring the success of your estate plan.

- **Yourself (as the initial trustee):** You maintain control of your assets while alive, but a successor trustee will take over after your passing or incapacity.
- **Successor Trustee:** A trusted individual who will step in to manage the trust upon your incapacity or death. This can be a family member, close friend, or professional fiduciary.
- **Corporate or Professional Trustee:** A bank or trust company that provides professional management services, ideal for

complex trusts or high-value estates. Professional trustees offer impartiality and expertise in financial management.

- **Co-Trustees:** Some individuals choose to name two trustees to work together in managing the trust, ensuring transparency, checks and balances, and diverse decision-making expertise.

While co-trustees can provide accountability and shared responsibility, they can also introduce challenges. Disagreements between co-trustees may delay decisions, especially when the trust does not clearly define how disputes should be resolved. Additionally, many financial institutions require both trustees to sign off on actions, such as accessing accounts or selling property, which can slow down administration or create logistical issues if one trustee is unavailable.

If you are considering co-trustees, it's important to choose individuals who communicate well, share similar values, and understand the responsibilities involved. In some cases, it may be more efficient to name a single trustee with a reliable successor.

STEP 5: DRAFT AND FORMALIZE THE TRUST DOCUMENT

Once you've determined your goals, assets, and trustees, you'll need to draft the legal document. While some individuals use DIY templates, consulting an estate planning attorney ensures your trust complies with all relevant laws. Key components of a trust document include:

- **Grantor's (your) name**
- **Beneficiaries and contingent beneficiaries**
- **Successor trustee designation and their responsibilities**

- **Distribution instructions for assets, including any conditions**
- **Special conditions or terms for asset protection or specific needs**
- **Instructions for handling taxes, debts, and legal matters**
- **Provisions for incapacity planning**

Once finalized, the document must be signed and **notarized** to be legally binding. It is advisable to maintain copies in a secure location and provide relevant parties with access to key documents.

STEP 6: FUNDING YOUR TRUST – WHAT ASSETS TO INCLUDE (AND HOW)

A common mistake is **failing to transfer assets into the trust**, which renders it ineffective. Here's how to fund your trust properly:

Real Estate and Property

- Change the title of any property to reflect the trust as the owner.

Before transferring your home or other real estate into a trust, it's important to review your **homeowners insurance and title insurance policies**, as well as your mortgage agreement. Some insurance companies require updated documentation when property ownership changes—even if the transfer is to your own trust.

In most cases, transferring a home to a **revocable living trust** does not trigger the "due-on-sale" clause in your mortgage, but it's still wise to notify your lender. Additionally, ensure your insurance provider is aware of the transfer and that the trust is named as an additional insured party if required.

Taking these steps helps maintain uninterrupted coverage and prevents potential claim issues down the line.

- File the updated deed with your county recorder's office.

Out-of-State Real Estate and Ancillary Probate

If you own property in more than one state, such as a vacation home or rental property, it's important to transfer **each property into your trust** individually. Otherwise, your estate could be subject to **ancillary probate**—a separate probate process required in every state where you own real estate.

This not only increases legal costs and delays but can also burden your beneficiaries with complex, multi-jurisdictional court proceedings. By retitling out-of-state real estate into your living trust, you ensure that **all properties are administered under one unified estate plan**, and your family can avoid multiple probate actions.

An estate planning attorney can help prepare the appropriate deeds and ensure that each transfer complies with the local property laws in that state.

- Ensure mortgages and liens are addressed when transferring real estate.

Bank Accounts and Investments

- Update account ownership or designate the trust as the **beneficiary**.

- Contact your financial institution to complete necessary paperwork.

• Review tax implications with an advisor before transferring investment accounts.

Retirement Accounts and Life Insurance Policies

• Do **not** transfer tax-advantaged accounts like IRAs and 401(k)s directly into a trust.

• Instead, designate the trust as a **primary or contingent beneficiary** to maintain tax benefits.

The SECURE Act and Retirement Account Beneficiaries

The **SECURE Act**, passed in 2019, significantly changed how inherited retirement accounts—such as IRAs and 401(k)s—are distributed. Most non-spouse beneficiaries must now **withdraw the entire account balance within 10 years** of the original owner's death. This can lead to unintended tax burdens if not planned for properly.

If you name a **trust** as the beneficiary of a retirement account, special care must be taken. The trust must meet strict IRS "look-through" requirements to avoid accelerated taxation. This includes:

• Naming only **individuals** (not charities or entities) as trust beneficiaries

• Ensuring the trust is **valid under state law** and **irrevocable** upon the account holder's death

• Providing trust documentation to the plan administrator by the IRS deadline

If these rules are not met, the retirement account may need to be distributed much faster—often immediately—resulting in a substantial tax hit.

Tip: Work with an estate planning attorney who understands the SECURE Act rules to structure your trust properly if it will hold retirement account proceeds.

Business Interests and Other Assets

- Transfer ownership of business shares into the trust.
- Assign personal property with a formalized asset schedule.
- Ensure intellectual property rights, royalties, or patents are legally transferred.
- Include digital assets, such as cryptocurrency and monetized online accounts, to prevent access issues after death.

📌 Don't forget: You can download a detailed Trust Funding Checklist in the Companion Toolkit (see Chapter 20).

To help you complete this process, you can download a **Trust Funding Checklist** in the Companion Toolkit at the end of this book (see Chapter 20).

THE POUR-OVER WILL – A SAFETY NET FOR YOUR TRUST

A pour-over will serves as an essential backup to your living trust, ensuring that any assets not properly transferred to your trust during your lifetime are "poured over" into it after your death. This safeguard document:

- Captures forgotten or newly acquired assets that weren't added to your trust

- Names guardians for minor children (something a trust alone cannot do)
- Provides instructions for personal items or sentimental possessions
- Acts as a safety net to prevent partial intestacy, where some assets follow state law rather than your wishes

Even with meticulous planning, it's common to overlook certain assets when funding your trust. A pour-over will ensures these assets still avoid probate by directing them into your existing trust structure.

FINALIZING AND MAINTAINING YOUR LIVING TRUST

A living trust is not a "set it and forget it" document. Life changes, and so should your trust.

Regular Reviews and Updates

Reassess your trust every few years or when major life events occur, such as:

- Marriage or divorce
- Birth of children or grandchildren
- Changes in financial status
- Acquisition of new assets
- Changes in state or federal tax laws

Amending vs. Restating Your Trust

- **Amendments** are suitable for small changes, such as adding a new beneficiary.

- **Restating the trust** is better for significant revisions, ensuring the document remains clear and legally sound.

Keeping Beneficiaries and Trustees Informed

- Provide copies of the trust to your **successor trustee**.
- Keep a record of important documents in a secure location.
- Communicate with beneficiaries to prevent misunderstandings.

CONCLUSION

Creating a living trust is a proactive step toward securing your financial legacy. By carefully designing, funding, and maintaining your trust, you can protect your assets, avoid probate, and ensure your loved ones are provided for according to your wishes.

Taking the time to set up a trust properly now will provide **long-term peace of mind** for both you and your heirs. The key is **not just creating the trust but keeping it up to date** to reflect your changing circumstances.

A well-maintained living trust is an essential component of any estate plan, ensuring a seamless transfer of wealth, protection from legal complications, and financial security for generations to come.

CHAPTER 5

TAX STRATEGIES & LIVING TRUSTS

ESTATE TAXES & YOUR TRUST – HOW TO MINIMIZE LIABILITIES

A well-structured living trust can help reduce or even eliminate estate taxes, ensuring that your beneficiaries receive the maximum possible inheritance while minimizing financial burdens. Understanding estate tax laws and incorporating tax-efficient strategies into your trust planning can significantly impact how much of your estate remains intact.

UNDERSTANDING ESTATE TAXES

Estate taxes, sometimes called the "death tax," are levied on the transfer of an individual's assets upon their passing. While federal estate tax only applies to estates exceeding a certain threshold (which changes annually), some states impose their own estate or inheritance taxes. These taxes can significantly erode the value of an estate if not properly managed, making tax planning essential.

State Estate and Inheritance Taxes

While the federal estate tax affects only the largest estates, many states impose their own estate or inheritance taxes—sometimes with much lower exemption thresholds. For example:

- **Massachusetts and Oregon**: Exemptions begin around **$1 million**

- **New York**: Approx. **$6.9 million exemption**, but "cliff tax" can result in a full tax if the estate slightly exceeds the threshold

- **Connecticut, Vermont, Washington, and Illinois**: Also have active estate tax systems

- **Pennsylvania and Nebraska**: Impose **inheritance taxes** based on the beneficiary's relationship to the decedent

Unlike estate taxes (paid by the estate), **inheritance taxes** are paid by the recipient of the inheritance. This can create unexpected costs for heirs, especially in blended or extended families.

Because state tax laws vary widely and change frequently, it's essential to consult a local estate planning attorney to ensure your trust strategy is optimized for your state's rules.

For 2023, the federal estate tax exemption stands at $13.99 million per individual ($27.98 million for married couples). However, assets above this threshold are taxed at a rate of up to 40%. Some states, including New York, Massachusetts, and Oregon, have lower exemption limits and additional state-level estate taxes. Understanding these limits can help individuals take proactive steps to mitigate potential tax burdens.

Under current law, the high federal estate tax exemption of $13.99 million per individual (and $27.98 million for married couples) is scheduled to **sunset at the end of 2025**. If Congress does not act, the exemption will revert to pre-2018 levels—approximately **$6–7 million per person** (adjusted for inflation).

This change could significantly impact families who previously assumed they were under the exemption threshold. Individuals with estates near or above the projected lower limits should consider advanced planning strategies to lock in the current exemption while it remains available. Trust structures like **credit shelter trusts, spousal lifetime access trusts (SLATs)**, or **gifting strategies** can help reduce exposure to future estate taxes.

THE IMPACT OF CHANGING ADMINISTRATIONS ON ESTATE TAX LAWS

Estate tax laws are subject to political shifts and frequently change with different presidential administrations and Congressional control. While this chapter reflects current exemptions and strategies, it's important to note that these thresholds may increase, decrease, or expire entirely with future legislation. What constitutes an effective tax-minimizing strategy today may need adjustment as laws evolve. This underscores the importance of regular trust reviews with your estate planning attorney and tax professional, ensuring your plan remains optimized regardless of legislative changes. A flexible trust structure can help your estate adapt to shifting tax environments while still achieving your wealth preservation goals.

HOW A LIVING TRUST CAN REDUCE ESTATE TAXES

- **Marital Deduction Trusts** – Assets transferred to a surviving spouse qualify for an unlimited marital deduction, deferring estate tax until the second spouse's passing.

- **Bypass Trusts (Credit Shelter Trusts)** – Allows couples to maximize their combined exemption, reducing estate tax liability.
- **Charitable Remainder Trusts** – Donating assets to a charitable trust can provide tax benefits and support philanthropic causes.
- **Irrevocable Life Insurance Trusts (ILITs)** – Ensures that life insurance proceeds are excluded from estate tax calculations.
- **Generation-Skipping Trusts (GSTs)** – Transfers wealth directly to grandchildren, bypassing one level of estate tax.
- **Qualified Terminable Interest Property (QTIP) Trusts** – Provides for a surviving spouse while ensuring that remaining assets pass to designated heirs, optimizing tax efficiency.
- **Grantor Retained Annuity Trusts (GRATs)** – Allows high-net-worth individuals to transfer appreciating assets at reduced gift tax rates.

INCOME TAX CONSIDERATIONS – UNDERSTANDING TAX IMPLICATIONS FOR YOUR TRUST

The taxation of trusts varies based on their structure. Revocable and irrevocable trusts are treated differently in terms of tax liability.

How Revocable & Irrevocable Trusts Differ in Taxation

- **Revocable Trusts:** The grantor retains control over trust assets, meaning income is reported on their personal tax return.
- **Irrevocable Trusts:** The trust is treated as a separate entity and taxed at trust tax rates, which can be higher than personal tax rates. High trust tax rates can necessitate strategic income distribution to beneficiaries.

Tax-Advantaged Strategies for Trusts

• **Grantor Retained Annuity Trusts (GRATs)** – Allows asset appreciation to transfer with reduced gift tax implications.

• **Qualified Personal Residence Trusts (QPRTs)** – Enables homeowners to transfer a residence to heirs while lowering gift tax liability.

• **Dynasty Trusts** – Passes wealth down multiple generations while avoiding estate taxes at each level.

• **Intentionally Defective Grantor Trusts (IDGTs)** – Removes assets from an estate while allowing the grantor to pay income taxes, reducing overall estate tax liability.

• **Charitable Lead Trusts (CLTs)** – Provides tax benefits while supporting charities before ultimately distributing assets to heirs.

GIFT TAX STRATEGIES – SMART GIFTING WHILE PROTECTING YOUR ASSETS

The IRS allows individuals to make tax-free gifts up to a certain limit each year. Understanding gift tax rules is key to effective estate planning.

Tax-Free Gifting Techniques

• **Annual Gift Exclusion** – Gifts up to the annual exclusion amount ($19,000 per recipient in 2025) are not subject to gift tax.

• **Lifetime Gift Exemption** – Allows tax-free gifts up to the federal exemption limit ($13.99 million in 2025).

• **529 College Savings Plans** – Contributions qualify as gifts but allow front-loading multiple years' worth of gifts.

- **Medical & Educational Exemptions** – Payments made directly to medical providers or educational institutions are exempt from gift tax limits.

- **Spousal Gifting Strategies** – Unlimited tax-free gifts between spouses who are both U.S. citizens.

- **Family Limited Partnerships (FLPs)** – Allows structured asset transfers while minimizing gift and estate taxes.

- **Irrevocable Gifting Trusts** – Establishes control over gifted assets while ensuring tax-efficient transfers.

TRUSTS AND LONG-TERM CARE PLANNING

While living trusts are often discussed in the context of tax efficiency and probate avoidance, they also play a vital role in long-term care planning—especially when it comes to preserving assets in the face of potential nursing home or assisted living costs.

The Cost of Long-Term Care

Long-term care can quickly deplete an estate. According to Genworth's 2024 Cost of Care Survey, the average cost of a private nursing home room in the U.S. exceeds $110,000 per year. Many families turn to Medicaid to cover these expenses, but qualifying requires careful advance planning.

Medicaid and the Lookback Period

Medicaid eligibility rules impose a five-year "lookback period" on asset transfers. That means if you transfer assets into a trust or give them away within five years of applying for Medicaid, those transfers can trigger penalties and delay eligibility.

This makes **timing essential**. A trust-based long-term care strategy must be implemented well in advance of any anticipated need for Medicaid.

The Role of Irrevocable Trusts

Revocable living trusts, while excellent for estate planning, **do not protect assets from Medicaid spend-down requirements**, because the grantor retains control. To protect assets for long-term care purposes, an **irrevocable Medicaid Asset Protection Trust (MAPT)** may be more appropriate.

Key features of a MAPT:

- Assets are no longer counted toward Medicaid eligibility
- The grantor cannot freely access the assets, but can usually continue to receive income from them (e.g., rent or dividends)
- Assets can be preserved for heirs
- The five-year lookback still applies, so early planning is critical

While irrevocable trusts reduce flexibility, they provide asset protection that revocable trusts cannot. They should only be created under the guidance of an experienced elder law or estate planning attorney.

Trust Planning Is Not a Complete Long-Term Care Strategy

It's important to understand that no trust alone guarantees full protection from nursing home costs. Trusts are just one part of a broader long-term care plan, which may also include:

- **Long-term care insurance**
- **Hybrid life insurance with long-term care riders** (offering both a death benefit and long-term care coverage)
- **Strategic spend-down planning** to reduce countable assets in a Medicaid-compliant way

- **Designated caregivers and powers of attorney** to manage care decisions

Balancing Control and Protection

A common mistake is waiting too long to begin long-term care planning, often out of fear of losing control over assets. But early planning can strike a balance:

- Use a **revocable trust** for most of your estate plan
- Consider transferring high-risk assets (like a second home or rental property) into an **irrevocable trust** early
- Retain sufficient liquid assets and income for lifestyle needs

Properly structured, this hybrid approach gives you flexibility now and protection later.

Professional Guidance Matters

Long-term care planning intersects estate law, tax law, and Medicaid rules—all of which vary by state and change frequently. An experienced elder law attorney can help you:

- Evaluate whether a MAPT makes sense for your situation
- Understand the tax consequences of transferring assets
- Navigate the lookback period without penalties
- Integrate long-term care into your broader estate plan

By planning ahead with the right type of trust, you can reduce financial risk, preserve assets for your family, and maintain more control over your care and legacy.

CONCLUSION

Effective tax planning with a living trust can significantly reduce the burden of estate, income, and gift taxes, preserving more wealth for your beneficiaries. A well-structured trust, combined with strategic gifting and tax-efficient planning, ensures that more of your hard-earned wealth remains within your family.

Working with an estate planning attorney or tax professional is crucial to ensure compliance with the latest tax laws and maximize the benefits of your trust structure. Tax regulations change frequently, and an expert can help navigate complex scenarios while optimizing your trust's tax position.

Proper planning today will ensure that your assets are distributed efficiently and in a tax-advantaged manner for generations to come. By proactively addressing estate, income, and gift tax considerations, you create a strong financial foundation that benefits your heirs and protects your legacy.

CHAPTER 6

KEEPING YOUR TRUST UP TO DATE

THE IMPORTANCE OF REGULAR REVIEWS AND UPDATES

A living trust is not a one-time document that you create and forget. Life is constantly changing, and your trust should reflect those changes to ensure your assets are protected and distributed according to your wishes. Regular reviews and updates help keep your trust current and effective, preventing unnecessary legal issues and complications for your heirs. Keeping your trust aligned with your current financial and personal circumstances ensures that your long-term estate planning goals remain intact.

Additionally, outdated trust provisions can cause confusion and disputes among beneficiaries, leading to costly legal battles. By periodically reviewing your trust, you can ensure that it remains a legally sound and reliable document that carries out your estate planning objectives efficiently.

WHEN TO REVIEW YOUR LIVING TRUST

You should review your trust periodically, especially when major life events occur. Consider updating your trust in the following situations:

- **Marriage or Divorce** – Adding or removing a spouse as a beneficiary or trustee. Changes in marital status can significantly impact asset distribution and inheritance rights.

- **Birth or Adoption of Children or Grandchildren** – Ensuring new family members are included in your estate plan and protected in case of unforeseen circumstances. Omitting a new family member from the trust could lead to unintended disinheritance.

- **Death of a Beneficiary or Trustee** – Updating named individuals in case of their passing to avoid disruptions in trust administration. If a trustee or key beneficiary passes away, the trust must be updated to reflect new appointments and inheritance adjustments.

- **Significant Changes in Financial Status** – Adjusting your asset distribution plan to reflect new wealth, business acquisitions, investments, or major financial losses. Major financial gains, such as an inheritance or lottery winnings, may require changes to trust allocations.

- **Relocation to a New State** – Different states have different estate laws; updating your trust ensures compliance with local regulations and maintains its enforceability. Some states have specific trust provisions that may impact how your estate is handled upon your passing.

- **Changes in Tax Laws** – Federal and state tax regulations evolve frequently, potentially impacting your estate and tax liability. A tax-efficient strategy should be reviewed periodically.

Tax laws regarding estate exemptions, deductions, and trust taxation can shift frequently, necessitating updates to ensure optimal estate tax planning.

- **Major Life Events for Beneficiaries** – If a beneficiary becomes disabled, financially unstable, or estranged, you may need to adjust their inheritance conditions or establish special trust provisions to protect them. Consider creating a special needs trust or limiting lump-sum distributions to ensure responsible management of assets.

AMENDING VS. RESTATING YOUR TRUST

When updating a living trust, you can either amend it or restate it. The choice depends on the extent of the changes required and the overall clarity of your existing trust document.

Amending Your Trust

A trust amendment is a legal document that modifies specific provisions of your trust without rewriting the entire document. Amendments are suitable for minor updates, such as:

- Adding or removing a beneficiary.
- Changing the successor trustee.
- Adjusting the distribution of specific assets.
- Modifying conditions for asset disbursement.

However, multiple amendments over time can make the trust difficult to interpret and may create confusion. If significant changes are needed or if amendments are stacking up, restating the trust might be a better option.

Restating Your Trust

A restatement is a complete revision of your living trust that replaces the original document while keeping the original date of establishment intact. This approach is beneficial when:

• Multiple amendments have made the trust document overly complex or contradictory.

• There are substantial changes to asset distribution, trustee designations, or special instructions.

• Legal language needs updating to comply with current estate laws, regulations, or tax strategies.

• Ensuring clarity for your successor trustee and beneficiaries to avoid legal disputes or misunderstandings.

Restating your trust ensures a clean, easy-to-understand document that remains legally enforceable and aligned with your evolving needs.

KEEPING BENEFICIARIES AND TRUSTEES INFORMED

Regular communication with beneficiaries and trustees helps prevent disputes and ensures that your trust operates smoothly when needed. Consider the following steps:

• **Provide a Copy of the Trust to Key Individuals** – Ensure your successor trustee has a copy of the trust and understands their responsibilities to avoid confusion when the trust becomes active.

• **Discuss Changes with Family Members** – Keeping beneficiaries informed about changes can prevent conflicts, misunderstandings, and legal disputes among family members. Transparency can help manage expectations and reduce the likelihood of future disagreements.

• **Store Documents Securely** – Keep the original trust document and any amendments in a secure, accessible location, such as a safe or with your attorney, while ensuring key individuals know how to access it when needed.

• **Designate a Digital Asset Plan** – Include online financial accounts, cryptocurrency, intellectual property, and other digital assets to ensure they are properly managed and transferred per your wishes. Without proper planning, digital assets may be inaccessible or lost entirely.

Ensuring Your Trust Reflects Your Wishes

An outdated trust may not provide the protection and benefits you originally intended. By regularly reviewing and updating your trust, you can:

• **Prevent Legal Challenges** – Keeping your trust up to date reduces the likelihood of disputes, probate issues, or court challenges from disinherited or confused heirs.

• **Optimize Tax Benefits** – Regular updates ensure that your trust takes advantage of current tax laws and estate planning strategies to minimize estate tax liability.

• **Align Your Legacy with Your Goals** – As your life and priorities evolve, so should your trust to reflect your legacy, philanthropic efforts, and financial aspirations.

• **Ensure Efficient Asset Transfer** – Avoid delays, legal complexities, and administrative issues by ensuring assets remain properly titled and allocated within the trust.

• **Enhance Trustee Oversight** – Regular reviews ensure that successor trustees are still appropriate for their roles and prepared to manage your estate when necessary.

Final Steps in Maintaining Your Trust

To keep your trust fully optimized, establish a schedule for periodic reviews and include professional oversight when necessary:

• **Set a Reminder to Review Annually** – Revisit your trust each year or every few years to ensure it still meets your goals.

• **Work with an Estate Planning Attorney** – Legal professionals can provide guidance on laws, tax planning, and complex trust structures. An attorney can also ensure that your trust remains legally valid in all relevant jurisdictions.

• **Coordinate with Financial Advisors** – Ensuring that investments, retirement accounts, and insurance policies align with your trust can provide additional security and long-term benefits. Regular financial reviews can help optimize wealth preservation strategies.

• **Keep Trust Assets Properly Titled** – Assets left out of a trust may still be subject to probate. Regularly verify that all applicable properties, accounts, and investments are titled appropriately.

• **Consider Successor Trustee Training** – If you have chosen a family member as a successor trustee, providing them with educational resources and training can help them manage the trust effectively when the time comes.

CONCLUSION

A living trust is a dynamic document that should evolve with your life circumstances. By periodically reviewing and updating your trust, you protect your assets, avoid unnecessary legal complications, and ensure your loved ones receive their inheritance as intended. Taking a proactive approach to maintaining your trust provides peace of mind for both you and your beneficiaries.

By keeping your trust updated, well-structured, and legally sound, you create a lasting framework that secures your financial legacy, minimizes complications, and ensures the smooth transition of your wealth to future generations. Regular maintenance and professional guidance ensure that your trust remains a powerful tool in protecting your estate and fulfilling your long-term objectives.

CHAPTER 7

POWERS OF ATTORNEY & HEALTHCARE DIRECTIVES

COMPLETING YOUR ESTATE PLAN BEYOND THE LIVING TRUST

While a living trust is an essential component of a well-crafted estate plan, it does not cover every situation—especially those involving healthcare or decisions outside of the assets placed in the trust. To ensure that your full range of financial, legal, and medical affairs is covered, you should also establish Powers of Attorney and healthcare directives. These documents complement your living trust and help provide complete protection during your lifetime, particularly in the event of incapacity.

WHAT A LIVING TRUST COVERS—AND WHAT IT DOESN'T

A living trust manages and distributes assets you place into it, both during your lifetime and after your death. However, it does not:

- Appoint someone to make medical decisions for you if you're incapacitated
- Manage non-trust assets unless retitled into the trust
- Allow someone to handle legal matters on your behalf unrelated to the trust

This is where Powers of Attorney and healthcare directives become essential.

TYPES OF POWERS OF ATTORNEY (POA)

1. Durable Financial Power of Attorney

This document allows you to name an agent (sometimes called an attorney-in-fact) to manage your financial affairs that fall outside your living trust. It remains in effect even if you become incapacitated.

Typical powers include:

- Paying bills and managing bank accounts
- Filing taxes
- Signing legal documents
- Handling retirement accounts or pensions not held in the trust
- Buying, selling, or managing real estate not titled in the trust

Without a POA, your family may need to go to court to obtain guardianship over your affairs, which is costly and time-consuming.

2. Limited or Springing Power of Attorney

These POAs are more specific:

• *Limited POA* grants authority for a specific task or time period (e.g., selling a property while you are abroad).

• *Springing POA* becomes active only upon a certain event, usually your incapacitation. These can be more difficult to use due to the need for medical confirmation of incapacity.

HEALTHCARE DIRECTIVES

1. Healthcare Power of Attorney (Medical POA)

This allows you to appoint someone to make medical decisions on your behalf if you're unable to communicate. This person may be asked to:

• Authorize surgery or medical treatment

• Approve or decline life support

• Coordinate care with your doctors

2. Living Will / Advance Healthcare Directive

This document outlines your preferences for medical treatment, especially in end-of-life scenarios.

You can specify:

• Whether you want life-sustaining treatment like feeding tubes or ventilators

• Preferences around pain relief and palliative care

• Organ donation wishes

These directives help avoid family conflict and ensure your wishes are known and respected.

WHY THESE DOCUMENTS MATTER

- **Avoid Court Intervention**: Without POAs or healthcare directives, your family may need to petition the court for guardianship or conservatorship.

- **Protect Your Wishes**: Medical and financial decisions can be made according to your instructions and values.

- **Reduce Burden on Loved Ones**: Appointing a trusted agent in advance removes guesswork and potential family conflict.

- **Complete Your Estate Plan**: Living trusts focus on assets; POAs and healthcare directives cover everything else.

BEST PRACTICES

- Keep copies of these documents with your trust and share them with your agents and medical providers.

- Review and update every few years, especially if your agent changes.

- Ensure your chosen agents are willing, trustworthy, and understand your wishes.

- Don't store these documents only in a safe deposit box—they need to be accessible in an emergency.

CONCLUSION

A comprehensive estate plan includes more than just a living trust. By also preparing a financial Power of Attorney, a healthcare Power of Attorney, and a living will, you ensure that your financial and medical needs are handled according to your wishes, even if you cannot advocate for yourself. These simple but powerful tools can protect you and your family during life's most vulnerable moments.

CHAPTER 8

PITFALLS & CHALLENGES OF LIVING TRUSTS

COMMON MISCONCEPTIONS ABOUT LIVING TRUSTS

While living trusts are an essential tool for estate planning, many individuals misunderstand their purpose and limitations. Some common misconceptions include:

• **A Living Trust Eliminates All Taxes** – While trusts can help with estate tax planning, they do not automatically remove all tax liabilities. Revocable living trusts retain the grantor's tax ID and are treated as the individual's property for tax purposes. Capital gains taxes typically apply only when appreciated assets are sold, not merely transferred. Proper structuring and guidance from a tax professional can help minimize overall tax burdens.

• **Trusts Are Only for the Wealthy** – Living trusts can benefit individuals of all income levels by simplifying asset distribution and avoiding probate. Even those with modest estates can use trusts to ensure efficient wealth transfer and avoid lengthy court processes. A trust is not just about wealth preservation; it is also about ensuring a smooth transition of assets without unnecessary legal intervention.

- **Once a Trust Is Created, It Requires No Further Action** – Trusts must be properly funded and periodically updated to remain effective. Changes in financial circumstances, family structures, and tax laws may necessitate modifications to your trust. Without proper funding, a trust is essentially a meaningless document.

- **All Assets Are Automatically Covered by a Trust** – A common mistake is assuming that once a trust is created, all assets are included. Assets must be properly titled in the trust's name to be protected. Some assets, such as retirement accounts, cannot be retitled but may list the trust as a beneficiary if appropriate. It is critical to regularly review and update asset ownership to ensure they are covered under the trust's provisions.

THE RISKS OF POOR PLANNING

Failing to plan properly can result in unintended consequences that undermine the benefits of a trust. Common pitfalls include:

- **Failing to Fund the Trust** – A trust is only effective if assets are properly transferred into it. Neglecting to retitle bank accounts, property, or investments means they could still be subject to probate. Many individuals create a trust but fail to move their assets into it, rendering it ineffective.

- **Naming the Wrong Trustee** – Selecting an inexperienced or untrustworthy trustee can lead to financial mismanagement or legal disputes. Trustees should have the knowledge, integrity, and financial acumen to administer the trust effectively. It is also wise to name a successor trustee in case the original trustee is unable to fulfill their duties.

• **Potential Complications with Multiple Co-Trustees** – Appointing more than one trustee can ensure checks and balances, but it may also lead to disagreements and delays in decision-making. Clear instructions on how disputes are resolved and who has authority in specific situations should be included in the trust document.

• **Not Updating the Trust Regularly** – Family circumstances, tax laws, and financial holdings evolve over time. Failing to review and amend a trust can result in outdated provisions that do not align with your wishes. A trust should be reviewed at least every three to five years, or whenever significant life changes occur.

• **Ignoring Tax Consequences** – Trusts must be structured with tax implications in mind to avoid unnecessary burdens on beneficiaries. Revocable living trusts do not reduce estate taxes on their own. Additional strategies, such as AB trusts or irrevocable trusts, may be necessary for tax mitigation. Consulting a tax professional ensures that your estate plan is as efficient as possible.

• **Relying Solely on a Trust Without Other Estate Planning Tools** – Trusts work best when combined with other estate planning measures, such as wills, powers of attorney, and healthcare directives. A pour-over will is often used to transfer any unfunded assets into the trust upon death. Some assets, such as retirement accounts, require specific beneficiary designations that cannot be managed through a trust.

• **Out-of-State Property Considerations** – Owning property in more than one state can complicate trust administration and tax obligations. It's essential to address how out-of-state real estate will be handled within the trust and to consider whether ancillary probate or separate legal filings may be necessary.

• **Digital Asset Planning** – Digital assets, such as email accounts, online banking, and cloud storage, may require specific language in a trust to ensure proper access and control. Including digital asset provisions helps trustees manage these assets legally and efficiently.

HIDDEN COSTS OF LIVING TRUSTS

While trusts provide numerous benefits, there are associated costs that individuals should be aware of, including:

• **Initial Legal Fees** – Drafting a living trust often requires legal assistance, which can be expensive, particularly for complex estates. Fees vary depending on the attorney's experience and the level of detail needed. For simpler estates, more affordable trust packages or templates may be an option, though legal review is still recommended.

• **Trust Administration Fees** – If a professional trustee is hired, ongoing management fees may apply. The cost can vary depending on the complexity of the trust and the services required. Professional trustees often charge an annual percentage of the trust's value for their services.

• **Potential Legal Disputes** – If a trust is not clearly written or updated, it may lead to legal challenges from beneficiaries. Ambiguous language or unclear directives can cause delays and costly litigation. Working with an attorney to draft clear provisions can help avoid future disputes.

• **Tax Implications** – While trusts can provide tax advantages, certain trust structures may trigger unintended tax liabilities.

For example, irrevocable trusts may have different tax filing requirements and responsibilities. Consulting a tax professional ensures that your trust is structured optimally.

• **Record-Keeping and Compliance Costs** – Maintaining a trust requires proper record-keeping and documentation of transactions. While revocable trusts generally do not require separate tax filings during the grantor's lifetime, trustees must still ensure compliance after death or with irrevocable trusts. This includes fulfilling fiduciary responsibilities and properly documenting asset distributions.

• **Potential Higher Property Insurance Costs** – Transferring real estate into a trust may impact your homeowner's insurance. Some insurance providers may require updated policies or treat the property differently once it's owned by a trust. It's important to notify your insurer and confirm continued coverage.

ENSURING A LIVING TRUST WORKS AS INTENDED

To maximize the effectiveness of a living trust and avoid costly mistakes, consider these steps:

• **Work with an Experienced Estate Planning Attorney** – Proper legal guidance ensures that the trust is structured correctly and adheres to applicable laws. Estate laws change frequently, and staying updated is crucial.

• **Fund the Trust Properly** – Ensure that real estate, financial accounts, and other assets are correctly titled in the trust's name. A trust without properly titled assets is ineffective. Updating account beneficiaries to align with the trust structure is also essential.

• **Review and Update Regularly** – Reassess the trust periodically to reflect changes in laws, finances, or family situations. Major life events such as marriage, divorce, birth, or death should trigger a review of your trust. Keeping the trust current reduces the risk of legal issues or unintended asset distribution.

• **Communicate with Beneficiaries and Trustees** – Clear instructions help prevent misunderstandings and legal conflicts. Informing trustees and beneficiaries about their roles and responsibilities fosters transparency and ensures a smooth transition when the trust is enacted. Providing a non-binding letter of intent with additional explanations can be beneficial.

• **Plan for Contingencies** – Life is unpredictable, and planning for potential scenarios such as disability, long-term care, or changes in beneficiary circumstances is essential to maintain the trust's effectiveness. Setting up provisions for guardianship or medical directives is highly recommended.

• **Integrate with Other Estate Planning Tools** – A trust should work alongside a will, powers of attorney, healthcare proxies, and beneficiary designations to ensure a comprehensive estate plan. No single tool can cover all aspects of estate planning, so a multi-faceted approach is necessary.

• **Consider Professional Trustees for Complex Estates** – If managing your trust seems too burdensome, a corporate trustee or financial institution can provide expert management services. This is especially useful for large estates or those requiring specialized investment management.

CONCLUSION

A well-structured living trust provides numerous benefits, but only if properly maintained and administered. Avoiding common pitfalls through proper planning, regular updates, and professional guidance ensures that your trust serves its intended purpose, protecting your legacy and benefiting your heirs.

By taking a proactive approach, reviewing your trust regularly, and working with experienced professionals, you can ensure that your estate plan remains current, legally sound, and aligned with your financial goals. A properly managed trust can save your heirs time, money, and stress while safeguarding your assets and legacy for future generations.

CASE STUDY: PROTECTING A SPECIAL NEEDS BENEFICIARY

James and Laura had two children, one of whom—Evan—was born with a developmental disability. As Evan grew older, they realized that leaving him a direct inheritance through a will could jeopardize his eligibility for Medicaid and other essential government benefits.

Working with an estate planning attorney, they created a revocable living trust and included a Special Needs Trust (SNT) as a subtrust specifically for Evan. This structure allowed them to provide for Evan's future without disqualifying him from vital public assistance.

When James and Laura passed away, the trustee allocated funds into Evan's SNT. These funds were used to supplement Evan's care—covering transportation, therapies, and personal needs—without affecting his eligibility for government programs.

Because the plan was thoughtfully crafted, the family avoided probate, ensured long-term support for Evan, and protected his public benefits. Their trust also reduced conflict by clearly defining how each child would be cared for.

This case illustrates how a living trust with a Special Needs Trust provision can provide peace of mind and lasting protection for vulnerable beneficiaries.

CHAPTER 9

TRUSTS FOR BLENDED FAMILIES

NAVIGATING COMPLEX FAMILY DYNAMICS WITH CLARITY AND CARE

Blended families are increasingly common, and they often bring unique challenges to estate planning. Whether you have stepchildren, are in a second marriage, or want to ensure children from a prior relationship are treated fairly, a well-structured living trust can provide clarity, fairness, and peace of mind.

THE CORE CHALLENGES IN BLENDED FAMILY PLANNING

Traditional estate planning assumes a straightforward nuclear family, but blended families may include:

- Children from previous marriages or relationships
- Stepchildren not legally adopted
- A spouse who is not the parent of all the children

• Unequal relationships or financial support among children

Without careful planning, these situations can lead to unintentional disinheritance, family conflict, or legal disputes after your death.

Common scenarios include:

• A surviving spouse remarries and leaves assets to their new family, cutting out your children

• Stepchildren unintentionally receive nothing because they're not legally your heirs

• One child receives a disproportionate share due to outdated documents or assumptions

HOW A LIVING TRUST CAN HELP

A revocable living trust allows you to:

• Direct how and when each beneficiary receives assets

• Protect assets for your biological children while still supporting a surviving spouse

• Prevent probate and reduce the risk of court battles

• Appoint a neutral trustee to fairly manage distributions if needed

Trusts offer far more flexibility than a simple will and allow you to structure your estate to reflect your exact wishes.

KEY STRATEGIES FOR BLENDED FAMILIES

1. Lifetime Use Rights for a Surviving Spouse

You can allow your spouse to live in the home or receive income from trust assets during their lifetime, while preserving the principal for your children.

Example: "My spouse may live in the home until death or remarriage. Upon that event, the home will be sold and proceeds distributed equally among my children."

2. Separate Trusts for Separate Assets

You can create one trust to provide for your spouse and another to benefit your children immediately, especially for assets you want passed directly to them.

3. QTIP Trusts (Qualified Terminable Interest Property Trusts)

These trusts provide income to your surviving spouse for life but ensure the remainder goes to your children. Useful for second marriages and larger estates.

4. Appointing a Professional Trustee

When family dynamics are sensitive, using a neutral third-party trustee (such as a bank or trust company) can reduce conflict and help enforce your instructions impartially.

5. Explicitly Name All Beneficiaries

Don't assume your stepchildren or biological children will be treated fairly by default. If you want a stepchild to inherit, they must be named in the trust.

COMMUNICATION IS KEY

One of the best ways to avoid future disputes is to communicate your intentions clearly while you're alive:

- Let your beneficiaries know what to expect

- Explain any unequal distributions
- Clarify that your plan is intentional and not the result of oversight or favoritism

Even if you choose not to share every detail, setting expectations can prevent confusion and resentment later.

CONCLUSION

Blended families require special care when it comes to estate planning. A living trust gives you the tools to honor your commitments to a spouse while protecting the inheritance of your children from a prior relationship. With thoughtful design, clear communication, and professional guidance, you can ensure that your wishes are respected and your family is supported—no matter how complex the dynamics may be.

CHAPTER 10

HOW A TRUST AFFECTS YOUR BENEFICIARIES

UNDERSTANDING BENEFICIARIES AND THEIR RIGHTS

A living trust provides a clear pathway for distributing assets to chosen individuals or organizations. Understanding the types of beneficiaries and the trustee's responsibilities is essential for ensuring a fair, lawful, and efficient distribution process.

Types of Beneficiaries

• **Primary Beneficiaries** – These individuals or entities receive distributions directly from the trust according to its terms.

• **Contingent Beneficiaries** – These parties inherit only if the primary beneficiaries are unable or unwilling to accept their share.

• **Residual Beneficiaries** – These beneficiaries receive any remaining trust assets after specific distributions have been made.

- **Special Needs Beneficiaries** – These beneficiaries require special consideration to avoid jeopardizing eligibility for government aid. A properly structured Special Needs Trust can preserve their access to benefits like Medicaid and SSI.

TAX IMPLICATIONS FOR BENEFICIARIES

Distributions from a trust may carry tax consequences, depending on the trust type and the nature of the assets. One key area of interest is the **step-up in basis** for inherited assets.

- **Revocable Trusts** – Assets in a revocable trust generally receive a step-up in basis to their fair market value at the time of the grantor's death. This helps reduce capital gains tax if the asset is later sold.

- **Irrevocable Trusts** – These trusts do not always receive a step-up in basis. The specific tax treatment can vary based on how the trust is structured and who is considered the owner of the assets for tax purposes.

It is essential to consult a tax professional to understand how a trust's structure will affect capital gains, income taxes, and estate tax obligations.

TRUSTEE LIMITATIONS: WHAT THEY CANNOT DO

While trustees are granted significant control, there are legal and ethical boundaries they must follow:

- They **cannot commingle trust assets with personal funds**.

- They **must avoid self-dealing**, unless explicitly authorized.

- They **cannot show favoritism** unless instructed by the trust terms.

- They **must act in the best interests of all beneficiaries**.

Failure to follow these rules can result in personal liability, removal from their role, and legal consequences.

PROTECTING BENEFICIARIES FROM LEGAL AND FINANCIAL RISKS

Trusts can provide robust protection for beneficiaries, particularly in situations involving divorce, lawsuits, or financial instability:

- **Divorce** – Assets held in a trust are often excluded from marital property division. However, this protection is typically **stronger with irrevocable trusts** than with revocable ones.

- **Creditors and Bankruptcy** – Trusts can shield a beneficiary's inheritance from creditor claims or bankruptcy proceedings, particularly when discretionary or spendthrift provisions are included.

- **Government Benefits** – Special Needs Trusts allow beneficiaries with disabilities to receive support without disqualifying them from essential aid programs.

THE IMPORTANCE OF SUCCESSOR BENEFICIARY DESIGNATIONS

Some trust structures rely on beneficiary designations for assets like retirement accounts, annuities, or life insurance policies. In these cases:

- It is crucial to name **both primary and successor beneficiaries** to ensure smooth transfer of assets.

- Failing to designate a successor can lead to **unintended consequences**, including probate or disputes.

Successor beneficiary planning is essential for continuity and to prevent gaps in distribution in the event a primary beneficiary passes away or disclaims their interest.

CONCLUSION: BALANCING RIGHTS AND PROTECTIONS

Beneficiaries of a trust have legal rights but also responsibilities. Trustees must honor the grantor's intent while protecting beneficiaries from legal, financial, and emotional harm. Understanding the nuanced ways a trust affects each beneficiary ensures a smoother administration and a more secure financial future for all involved.

CHAPTER 11

DIGITAL ASSETS & MODERN TRUST PLANNING

INTRODUCTION: THE DIGITAL SHIFT IN ESTATE PLANNING

As our lives become increasingly digital, so do our assets. From cryptocurrency and online investment accounts to photo libraries, email, social media, and virtual property, digital assets are now a key part of modern estate planning. Trusts must evolve to account for these non-tangible, often overlooked components of wealth. This chapter explores how digital assets are treated in trust planning, along with the strategies, tools, and precautions needed to safeguard and transfer them.

WHAT ARE DIGITAL ASSETS?

Digital assets encompass a wide range of online and electronic items with personal or financial value, including:

- Cryptocurrency (e.g., Bitcoin, Ethereum)
- NFTs (non-fungible tokens)

- Online banking and investment accounts
- Cloud storage files (documents, photos, videos)
- Email accounts and communications
- Social media accounts (Facebook, Instagram, Twitter/X)
- Domain names and websites
- Streaming services and digital libraries (eBooks, music, videos)
- Loyalty/rewards programs (e.g., airline miles, hotel points, credit card rewards)

Many of these assets carry real-world value and should not be excluded from your trust.

CRYPTOCURRENCY AND BLOCKCHAIN-BASED ASSETS

Handling Digital Currency in a Trust

Cryptocurrency is uniquely challenging to manage in a trust because of its decentralized nature and security requirements.

- **Cold storage options** – Consider storing crypto in offline wallets (hardware wallets or paper wallets) for enhanced security.
- **Seed phrase protection** – Trustees should only receive access to seed phrases or private keys under strict, documented protocols. Mismanagement of these can lead to permanent loss of assets.
- **Hardware security keys** – These add an extra layer of security and are strongly recommended for managing access to important crypto accounts.

Tax Reporting Complexities

Cryptocurrency transactions are subject to IRS reporting rules. Trustees and beneficiaries must:

- **Track cost basis** for every transaction, which can be difficult across multiple wallets and exchanges.
- Understand how to report **capital gains and losses**.
- Address special cases like **airdrops and hard forks**, which may be considered taxable events.

Failure to report crypto properly can lead to penalties or audits. Work with a CPA experienced in digital assets.

Valuation at Death

Establishing the fair market value of cryptocurrency and NFTs at the date of the grantor's death is crucial for estate tax purposes. Due to volatility, a qualified appraiser or digital asset specialist may be needed.

TRUSTS AND DIGITAL PLATFORM LIMITATIONS

A major hurdle in digital estate planning is the potential conflict between trust instructions and the **Terms of Service Agreements (TOS)** of digital platforms.

- Some providers **prohibit access** to a deceased person's account—even with legal documentation.
- Others may limit the trustee's ability to transfer ownership or access data.

To navigate this:

- Use built-in legacy tools when available (e.g., Google's Inactive Account Manager, Facebook's Legacy Contact).

• Store login credentials securely with the trust documentation.

• Include language in the trust that specifically **authorizes digital account access**.

PERIODIC REVIEW AND LEGAL COMPLIANCE

Digital asset laws and technology are evolving rapidly. To stay compliant:

• Review and update digital asset provisions in the trust **at least every 2–3 years**.

• Monitor changes in **state and federal laws** related to digital privacy, data access, and crypto regulation.

• Consider consulting legal experts who specialize in digital estate planning.

SECURITY MEASURES FOR DIGITAL TRUST ASSETS

Keeping digital assets secure is critical. Recommended strategies include:

• Use of **hardware wallets** and cold storage for crypto.

• **Password managers** to organize and share access.

• **Two-factor authentication (2FA)** for all linked accounts.

• **Hardware security keys** (e.g., YubiKey) for added protection of email, financial platforms, and crypto exchanges.

• **Encrypted backups** of trust documentation and access credentials stored in multiple secure locations.

LEGAL ACCESS TO DIGITAL ASSETS

Most states have adopted a law called the **Revised Uniform Fiduciary Access to Digital Assets Act (RUFADAA)**, which governs how trustees, executors, and agents can access digital property such as email accounts, cloud storage, cryptocurrency wallets, and social media profiles.

Under RUFADAA, access is not automatically granted—even if someone is named as trustee or agent in your estate plan. To ensure proper access:

- Your trust documents (and power of attorney) should **explicitly authorize digital asset access**.
- You may need to **use each platform's internal settings** to grant legacy access (e.g., Facebook's Legacy Contact or Google's Inactive Account Manager).
- Keep a secure, updated inventory of digital accounts and passwords using a password manager or encrypted file.

Without proper legal and practical preparation, your trustee could face significant delays or denial of access, even with a court order. Including clear digital asset instructions in your estate plan is critical in today's online world.

CONCLUSION: STAYING AHEAD IN A DIGITAL WORLD

As digital property grows in importance, it demands the same level of attention as traditional assets in estate planning. A trust that accounts for these assets ensures smoother administration and prevents permanent loss. With proper security, documentation, and legal planning, digital assets can be safely passed on to beneficiaries—just like any physical investment or heirloom.

The digital landscape is constantly shifting, and so should your estate plan. Revisit your trust regularly, consult professionals familiar with emerging technology, and take a proactive approach to digital legacy planning.

CHAPTER 12
TRUST ADMINISTRATION AFTER DEATH

WHAT HAPPENS WHEN THE GRANTOR PASSES – THE PROCESS UNFOLDS

A living trust is designed to function seamlessly upon the death of the grantor, ensuring that assets are transferred efficiently without the delays and expenses of probate. Unlike a will, which must go through a court-supervised process, a properly funded trust allows for immediate administration and asset distribution according to the grantor's instructions. However, the trustee plays a critical role in overseeing the execution of the trust and handling financial and legal responsibilities.

The transition of control from the grantor to the trustee is a legally significant process that requires careful planning, communication, and financial oversight. Trustees must understand their responsibilities, ensure that assets are handled appropriately, and address any legal or tax implications that may arise during the administration of the trust. A failure to administer the trust properly can result in disputes, delays, and even personal liability for the trustee.

KEY STEPS IN TRUST ADMINISTRATION

1 Locate and Review the Trust Document – The trustee must obtain the official trust document and review its provisions to understand their legal duties, responsibilities, and limitations.

2 Obtain the Death Certificate – Most financial institutions, government agencies, and property title offices require an official death certificate before releasing assets. Trustees should request multiple certified copies to expedite the process.

3 Obtain an EIN for the Trust – After the grantor's death, particularly for revocable trusts that become irrevocable, the trustee must apply for a new tax ID number (Employer Identification Number) to use in trust tax filings.

4 Notify Beneficiaries – The trustee must inform all designated beneficiaries about the trust's terms and their inheritance rights. This step should be handled carefully to minimize confusion, set expectations, and prevent potential disputes.

5 Identify and Secure Trust Assets – Trustees must locate and protect all trust assets, including real estate, bank accounts, investment portfolios, digital assets, and personal property. If necessary, they should re-title assets in the name of the trust for efficient management.

6 Set Up a Trust Bank Account – To manage trust-related transactions, a trustee should open a dedicated account for deposits, distributions, and expense payments. Keeping personal and trust funds separate is essential for financial transparency and legal compliance.

7 Pay Outstanding Debts and Taxes – The trustee must ensure that any outstanding debts, mortgages, final medical bills, and liabilities are settled before asset distribution. Ignoring debts can lead to legal claims against the estate.

8 File Necessary Tax Returns – Depending on the estate's size, tax filings may include federal estate taxes, state inheritance taxes, and final income tax returns. Trustees may need to work with tax professionals to ensure proper reporting.

9 Handle Investment Management – If the trust holds stocks, mutual funds, real estate, or other investment assets, the trustee must decide whether to liquidate or maintain them based on the trust's provisions and beneficiaries' best interests. Investments must be managed prudently to preserve value and comply with the trust's purpose.

10 Distribute Assets According to the Trust Terms – The trustee follows the trust's instructions to distribute funds or property to beneficiaries, adhering to any conditions, milestone-based distributions, or staggered payments. Failure to follow these terms precisely can result in legal action.

11 Final Accounting and Trustee Discharge – A final accounting should be prepared showing all trust activity and distributed to beneficiaries. Once reviewed and approved, trustees may obtain written releases or court approval to formally discharge their duties.

Each step requires careful documentation, financial oversight, and adherence to legal requirements to ensure that the trust administration proceeds smoothly and aligns with the grantor's wishes. Trustees who do not fulfill their responsibilities properly can be held legally liable, leading to fines, lawsuits, or removal from their role.

TIMELINE EXPECTATIONS FOR TRUST ADMINISTRATION

Trust administration can vary widely in duration depending on the complexity of the trust. General timeframes are as follows:

• **First 1–3 months** – Secure documents, notify beneficiaries, obtain EIN, and take possession of assets.

• **3–6 months** – Pay debts, determine tax liabilities, and begin asset appraisals.

• **6–12 months** – File tax returns, distribute preliminary assets, resolve disputes.

• **12–18+ months** – Final distributions, accounting, and trust closure.

Delays may occur with real estate sales, pending lawsuits, or tax audits, so setting realistic expectations with beneficiaries is important.

TRUSTEES: ROLES AND RESPONSIBILITIES IN FINALIZING THE ESTATE

The trustee is the individual or institution responsible for carrying out the trust's provisions. Their fiduciary duty requires them to act in the best interests of the beneficiaries, ensuring fair and lawful administration.

Duties of a Trustee

• **Upholding the grantor's wishes** – The trustee must execute the trust exactly as the grantor outlined, without modification or personal bias.

• **Managing financial transactions** – Trustees handle bill payments, outstanding loans, and investment management during the administration period.

• **Providing financial transparency** – Detailed records must be kept to ensure fair and legal administration of funds and distributions. Beneficiaries have the right to request reports on trust activities.

• **Acting impartially** – If multiple beneficiaries exist, the trustee must act neutrally and not favor one beneficiary over another.

• **Overseeing distributions** – Assets must be distributed at the correct time, whether in a lump sum, staggered distributions, or milestone-based disbursements.

• **Handling disputes** – If disagreements arise among beneficiaries, the trustee may need to mediate or seek legal guidance. Poor communication or mismanagement can result in lawsuits and removal of the trustee.

When a Professional Trustee May Be Necessary

A professional trustee may be appropriate when:

• The trust holds **complex assets** like businesses, commercial real estate, or international accounts.

• There are **family tensions or conflicting beneficiaries**.

• The trust is designed to last for many years or across multiple generations.

• The named trustee is **unwilling, unable, or unqualified** to serve.

Professional trustees can offer expertise, neutrality, and continuity.

HOW TAXES AFFECT TRUST ADMINISTRATION

Trust administration involves settling any outstanding tax obligations before assets can be fully distributed to beneficiaries. Taxes may include:

Federal and State Estate Taxes

• **Federal estate tax applies to estates exceeding $13.99 million (2025 exemption limit)** – Trustees must ensure that any owed estate tax is calculated and paid before distributing assets.

• **Note** – This exemption is scheduled to significantly decrease in **2026** unless new legislation is passed.

• **State inheritance taxes vary by location** – Some states impose separate inheritance taxes that may require additional filings.

• **Tax-efficient planning can help** – If the estate is subject to taxation, strategic asset liquidation or installment payments may be necessary to avoid penalties.

INCOME TAX CONSIDERATIONS

• **Final Personal Income Tax Return** – The trustee must file the deceased grantor's final income tax return (Form 1040) for the year of death.

• **Fiduciary Income Tax Return** – If the trust generates income (interest, dividends, rental income), a separate tax return (Form 1041) may be required.

• **Step-Up in Basis for Inherited Assets** – Beneficiaries may receive a tax advantage through the step-up in cost basis, reducing capital gains tax on inherited property.

Proper tax handling ensures that the trust remains in compliance with federal and state tax regulations, avoiding penalties and legal complications. Trusts with complex assets or international holdings may require specialized tax planning.

TRUST PROTECTORS AND ADVISORS

Trust protectors or advisors may be included in a trust to provide oversight and flexibility. They can:

• **Remove or replace the trustee** if misconduct or incapacity occurs.

• **Resolve disputes** without court involvement.

• **Modify administrative provisions** in response to legal or tax changes.

This added layer of support can preserve the trust's integrity and reduce litigation risks.

TRUSTEE COMPENSATION

Trustees are typically entitled to **reasonable compensation** for their time and effort. This can be based on:

• A **percentage of trust assets** (e.g., 0.5%–1.5% annually).

• An **hourly rate** for time spent administering the trust.

• A **flat fee** outlined in the trust document.

Family trustees often waive compensation, while professional trustees charge according to industry standards. Compensation must be disclosed to beneficiaries and documented clearly.

CONCLUSION

Trust administration after death is a detailed and legally significant process that requires careful planning, financial management, and adherence to legal obligations. A well-managed trust ensures that assets are preserved, financial obligations are met, and family members are provided for without unnecessary legal complications. By following proper procedures, trustees can protect the grantor's legacy while fulfilling their legal and financial responsibilities.

CHAPTER 13
AVOIDING COMMON TRUST ADMINISTRATION MISTAKES

INTRODUCTION: THE IMPORTANCE OF PROPER TRUST ADMINISTRATION

A living trust is only as effective as the way it is managed after the grantor's passing. While trusts are designed to simplify the transfer of assets and avoid probate, poor administration can lead to delays, legal disputes, tax complications, and financial loss for beneficiaries. Many common mistakes occur because trustees are unaware of their responsibilities, fail to follow legal and financial requirements, or mismanage assets due to lack of experience.

A trustee is not just a financial manager but also a legal representative, tax filer, and often a mediator among beneficiaries. Without a proper understanding of their role, even well-intentioned trustees can make errors that result in financial penalties, family disputes, or lawsuits. In this chapter, we will explore the most frequent mistakes made during trust administration and how to avoid them. Whether you are a trustee overseeing a trust for the first time or a beneficiary ensuring that your inheritance is handled properly, understanding these pitfalls can help ensure a smooth, legally compliant, and conflict-free trust administration process.

MISTAKE #1: FAILING TO PROPERLY FUND THE TRUST

Why It's a Problem:

A trust must be properly funded to function as intended. Many people set up a living trust but fail to transfer their assets into it. When assets remain titled in the grantor's name, they may still be subject to probate, negating one of the primary benefits of a trust. Unfunded or partially funded trusts often create confusion, legal delays, and unintended asset distribution outcomes.

How to Avoid It:

• Ensure that real estate, bank accounts, investment portfolios, and personal property are retitled in the name of the trust.

• Update beneficiary designations for retirement accounts and life insurance policies to align with the trust's estate planning strategy.

• Create an asset schedule listing all property included in the trust to avoid confusion and ensure that nothing is overlooked.

• Regularly review trust funding to incorporate newly acquired assets and ensure they are properly titled.

• Work with financial institutions to confirm that all accounts and investments reflect the trust as the owner or beneficiary.

• Avoid 'forgotten assets' by keeping a record of digital assets, online accounts, cryptocurrency wallets, and other intangible assets.

MISTAKE #2: MISUNDERSTANDING THE TRUSTEE'S DUTIES

Why It's a Problem:

Many trustees underestimate the level of responsibility and legal duty involved in administering a trust. A trustee is a fiduciary, meaning they have a legal obligation to act in the best interests of the beneficiaries. Mistakes such as mismanaging investments, failing to communicate with beneficiaries, or engaging in conflicts of interest can result in legal liability and financial consequences.

How to Avoid It:

• Understand fiduciary responsibilities – Trustees must act in good faith, manage trust assets prudently, and avoid self-dealing.

• Avoid commingling trust assets with personal funds, which is a breach of fiduciary duty and a common source of legal disputes.

• Seek professional guidance – Hiring an estate attorney or financial advisor can help ensure compliance with trust laws and protect the trustee from liability.

• Maintain accurate records – Keep detailed logs of all transactions, distributions, and decisions related to the trust.

• Document every distribution with receipts or written confirmation to maintain a clear audit trail.

• Avoid premature or improper distributions before debts, taxes, and expenses are settled.

• Diversify investments appropriately to reflect the trust's goals and risk tolerance. Failing to do so may violate the "Prudent Investor Rule."

• Disclose and address any potential conflicts of interest, especially if the trustee is also a beneficiary.

MISTAKE #3: DELAYING TRUST ADMINISTRATION

Why It's a Problem:

After the grantor passes, the trustee must act promptly to secure assets, notify beneficiaries, and begin administering the trust. Delays can cause financial difficulties for beneficiaries, create tax complications, and lead to disputes. If assets are left unmonitored, they may lose value, incur avoidable taxes, or become vulnerable to fraud.

How to Avoid It:

• Notify beneficiaries as soon as possible to manage expectations and outline the trust's distribution plan.

• Open a trust bank account to manage transactions and prevent co-mingling of personal and trust funds.

• Work with professionals (attorneys, accountants) to ensure that tax filings and other legal requirements are met promptly.

• Identify and secure trust assets immediately to prevent loss or unauthorized access.

• Schedule regular progress updates with beneficiaries to keep them informed.

• If real estate is part of the trust, arrange for property management or sale promptly to prevent deterioration or loss of value.

• Ensure all trust property is adequately insured against loss, damage, or liability.

MISTAKE #4: POOR COMMUNICATION WITH BENEFICIARIES

Why It's a Problem:

Beneficiaries may feel distrustful or frustrated if they do not receive timely updates about the trust's administration. Lack of transparency can lead to misunderstandings, disputes, and legal challenges. Trustees who fail to communicate clearly can be accused of mishandling funds or favoring certain beneficiaries over others.

How to Avoid It:

• Provide regular updates on the trust's status, expected timelines for distributions, and any delays that may arise.

• Be transparent about trust expenses and management decisions.

• Hold a formal meeting with beneficiaries to review the trust's provisions and address any concerns.

• Provide a written summary of trust administration activities to prevent miscommunication.

• Encourage open dialogue to prevent resentment and confusion among beneficiaries.

• Document all beneficiary communications in case of future disputes.

MISTAKE #5: FAILING TO PAY TRUST DEBTS AND TAXES

Why It's a Problem:

Before distributing assets, the trustee is responsible for ensuring that the trust's debts, final expenses, and taxes are paid. If these obligations are ignored, creditors or tax authorities may place claims against the trust.

How to Avoid It:

- File the grantor's final income tax return and settle any outstanding tax liabilities.

- Identify and pay off debts before distributing funds to beneficiaries.

- Work with a tax professional to ensure compliance with federal and state tax laws.

- Review estate tax exemption limits to determine if federal or state estate tax applies.

- Ensure that all property tax obligations are addressed if the trust includes real estate holdings.

- Check for medical bills and outstanding loans that must be paid before closing the trust.

MISTAKE #6: FAILING TO IDENTIFY AND PROPERLY VALUE TRUST ASSETS

Why It's a Problem:

If a trustee fails to locate or accurately value all trust assets, they risk mismanaging the estate, underpaying taxes, or distributing assets inequitably. This can lead to delays, legal challenges, and accusations of negligence.

How to Avoid It:

• Conduct a thorough inventory of all trust assets, including real property, personal items, financial accounts, business interests, and digital assets.

• Obtain formal appraisals or valuations for any significant assets, especially for estate tax purposes.

• Keep detailed records of valuations and update asset values as needed.

CONCLUSION: BEST PRACTICES FOR SUCCESSFUL TRUST ADMINISTRATION

Avoiding common mistakes requires education, organization, and professional support. By understanding their fiduciary responsibilities, communicating openly with beneficiaries, and properly managing assets, trustees can ensure a smooth, efficient, and legally compliant trust administration process.

Key Takeaways:

• A trust must be properly funded to function as intended.

• Trustees have a fiduciary duty to act in the best interests of beneficiaries.

• Avoid conflicts of interest and manage investments prudently.

• Timely administration prevents legal and financial complications.

• Clear communication reduces the risk of disputes.

• Tax planning is essential to preserve the value of the trust.

- Proper documentation helps avoid future legal challenges.
- Maintain insurance coverage for trust property.
- Finalizing the trust correctly is necessary to fulfill legal obligations.
- Seeking professional guidance can help navigate complex trust administration issues.

By proactively addressing these issues, trustees can protect the grantor's legacy, ensure fairness for beneficiaries, and successfully carry out their responsibilities.

CHAPTER 14
TRUST MODIFICATIONS, AMENDMENTS, AND TERMINATIONS

INTRODUCTION: UNDERSTANDING TRUST FLEXIBILITY

While living trusts provide stability and legal protection, they are not always set in stone. Life circumstances change, financial needs evolve, and tax laws are updated, making it necessary for grantors or trustees to modify or even terminate a trust. The ability to adapt a trust ensures that it continues to serve its intended purpose effectively. However, improper modifications can lead to legal disputes, tax complications, and unintended consequences for beneficiaries.

A trust modification may be a simple change, such as updating a beneficiary, or a complex revision requiring extensive legal adjustments. In many cases, trusts need periodic reviews to ensure they remain legally valid, tax-efficient, and aligned with the grantor's objectives. Whether the goal is to accommodate new family members, change asset distributions, or dissolve a trust entirely, understanding when, why, and how to make modifications is critical.

This chapter explores how and when to modify, amend, or terminate a living trust, the legal steps involved, and best practices to ensure compliance and clarity. Proper understanding of these procedures can help protect assets, minimize disputes, and maintain the integrity of the grantor's intentions.

WHEN AND WHY A TRUST MAY NEED TO BE MODIFIED

Common Reasons for Modifications

• **Changes in family circumstances** – Marriage, divorce, birth of children, or the death of a beneficiary or trustee may require an update.

• **Financial shifts** – A significant increase or decrease in assets, business ownership changes, or the need for additional financial protections.

• **Tax law changes** – Updates in estate tax laws may necessitate modifications to ensure optimal tax benefits and minimize liabilities.

• **Health concerns and incapacity planning** – The need to adjust medical directives, provide for long-term care, or appoint a new successor trustee.

• **Adjustments in beneficiary needs** – If a beneficiary becomes disabled, financially irresponsible, or experiences other major life events that affect inheritance planning.

• **Updating distribution terms** – If a grantor wants to change when and how beneficiaries receive their inheritance, such as implementing staggered payments instead of lump sums.

- **Fixing mistakes or clarifying ambiguous terms** – Sometimes, trust language needs to be revised to avoid conflicts, legal uncertainty, or misinterpretation.

- **Adding or removing trustees** – If a trustee can no longer serve or is no longer trusted to manage the trust effectively, an update is required.

- **Merging or splitting trusts** – Combining multiple trusts for efficiency or separating one trust into multiple trusts to better meet beneficiaries' needs.

- **Protecting digital assets and intellectual property** – Updating the trust to include cryptocurrency, digital wallets, domain names, royalties, or other intangible assets.

TYPES OF TRUST MODIFICATIONS

1 Minor Amendments – Simple updates like adding a beneficiary, changing a trustee, or adjusting distribution percentages.

2 Comprehensive Restatements – A full revision of the trust document, often used when multiple amendments make the trust difficult to interpret.

3 Court-Ordered Modifications – In some cases, a court may be required to approve changes, especially in irrevocable trusts.

4 Decanting – A process of transferring assets from one trust into another, typically with more favorable or updated terms. This is a growing trend in modern trust law, especially for modifying irrevocable trusts without court approval.

THE DIFFERENCE BETWEEN AMENDING AND RESTATING A TRUST

Trust Amendments: Making Minor Changes

A trust amendment is used when a grantor wants to modify specific terms without altering the entire document. This is a practical option when making small, straightforward changes such as:

- Updating successor trustees.
- Adjusting beneficiary distributions.
- Changing asset management instructions.
- Adding new terms to reflect recent life events.

Benefits of an Amendment:

- Simple and cost-effective.
- Keeps the existing trust document intact.
- Avoids unnecessary legal fees and retitling of assets.

Trust Restatements: Comprehensive Overhauls

A trust restatement replaces the existing trust document while maintaining its original creation date. This is recommended when:

- Multiple amendments have made the trust confusing or difficult to interpret.
- Major revisions are needed due to financial or personal circumstances.
- The grantor wants to modernize the trust language to comply with current laws.

- Reducing the risk of legal disputes over inconsistent amendments.
- Avoiding the hassle of retitling trust assets, as restatements do not require assets to be transferred again.

Why Choose a Restatement Instead of an Amendment?

- Prevents confusion from multiple amendments.
- Ensures consistency across all trust provisions.
- Preserves the trust's history while implementing significant updates.

TRUST TERMINATION PROCEDURES

Despite being less common, some trusts need to be fully terminated. A trust may be terminated when:

- The grantor revokes a revocable trust.
- All trust purposes have been fulfilled or are no longer achievable.
- Trust assets have been fully distributed.
- A court orders termination based on changed circumstances.

Termination Process:

- Confirm all debts and taxes have been paid.
- Provide beneficiaries with a final accounting.
- Execute a formal trust termination document.
- Notify relevant financial institutions.
- Close all trust accounts and obtain written releases if appropriate.

TAX CONSIDERATIONS WHEN MODIFYING A TRUST

When making modifications, especially to irrevocable trusts, grantors and trustees must consider potential tax consequences. Changes may:

- Affect the trust's **grantor or non-grantor status**, leading to different income tax treatments.
- Trigger **gift or generation-skipping transfer taxes** if asset control or beneficiary designations are altered.
- Impact **capital gains tax** strategies depending on how distributions or trust terms are updated.

Consult with a tax attorney or CPA before making significant changes to ensure compliance and avoid unintended tax consequences.

ROLE OF TRUST PROTECTORS IN FACILITATING MODIFICATIONS

A trust protector is an appointed individual or entity with limited powers to oversee and adjust the trust. These provisions are especially helpful for:

- Approving amendments without court involvement.
- Replacing trustees.
- Making administrative changes if tax laws change.

Having a trust protector adds flexibility and can reduce future legal costs.

COURT PETITIONS AND THE "MATERIAL PURPOSE" DOCTRINE

In some jurisdictions, modifying or terminating an irrevocable trust requires court approval. Courts typically assess whether:

- The **material purpose** of the trust would be frustrated by the proposed change.
- All beneficiaries consent to the modification.
- Circumstances have changed to such a degree that the original purpose can no longer be fulfilled.

This doctrine plays a critical role in judicial decision-making around irrevocable trust changes. Petitioners should be prepared to demonstrate why the change is necessary and how it aligns with or no longer serves the trust's original intent.

STATE-SPECIFIC CONSIDERATIONS

Trust laws and modification procedures vary significantly by state. Some states:

- Allow broader decanting powers.
- Require formal court approval for nearly all irrevocable trust changes.
- Impose unique witness or notarization requirements.
- Recognize "non-judicial settlement agreements" for simplified modifications.

Always consult an estate planning attorney familiar with your state's laws before making any changes to a trust.

CONCLUSION: KEEPING YOUR TRUST UPDATED AND EFFECTIVE

Trust modifications, amendments, and terminations are essential tools to ensure that a trust remains aligned with the grantor's wishes, financial goals, and legal requirements. Whether making minor changes or completely restating a trust, following proper legal steps can prevent disputes, protect assets, and maintain trust integrity.

Key Takeaways:

- Review your trust regularly to ensure it reflects your current situation.
- Use amendments for minor updates and restatements for major revisions.
- Understand the legal limits of modifying irrevocable trusts.
- Be aware of tax consequences that may arise from modifications.
- Trust protectors can provide flexibility and avoid court involvement.
- State laws vary, so work with legal professionals familiar with your jurisdiction.
- When needed, use decanting or court petitions to address irrevocable trust challenges.
- Consider the material purpose of the trust before requesting a modification.

By staying proactive, trustees and grantors can ensure that their trusts remain effective, enforceable, and aligned with their evolving needs.

CASE STUDY: PLANNING FOR A BLENDED FAMILY

After remarrying in his early 60s, David wanted to ensure both his new wife, Karen, and his two adult children from a previous marriage were fairly treated in his estate plan. He owned a home, several retirement accounts, and a small business.

David created a revocable living trust that outlined a clear, phased plan. Upon his death, Karen would have the right to live in the family home for the rest of her life, but the home would ultimately pass to his children. The trust also provided Karen with income from investments during her lifetime while preserving the principal for his children. His business interest was directed to his son, who had worked with him for years.

Because these details were built into the trust, there was no confusion or conflict after David's death. His children knew their inheritance was secure, and Karen felt financially supported without tension.

This case demonstrates how living trusts can thoughtfully navigate the complexities of blended families, preserving relationships while honoring the grantor's intentions.

CHAPTER 15

SPECIAL CONSIDERATIONS FOR COMPLEX TRUSTS

INTRODUCTION: THE ROLE OF COMPLEX TRUSTS IN ESTATE PLANNING

While basic living trusts serve as effective estate planning tools, complex trusts provide additional layers of protection, tax advantages, and asset management flexibility. Complex trusts often involve multiple beneficiaries, unique asset types, international considerations, or highly specific distribution instructions. These trusts can be designed to manage wealth for generations, shield assets from legal claims, or provide structured charitable giving.

Understanding how to properly manage and administer these trusts is essential to ensure compliance with legal requirements and the grantor's wishes. Trustees, attorneys, and financial advisors must work together to ensure that trust terms align with long-term goals while avoiding legal pitfalls and tax inefficiencies.

This chapter explores the different types of complex trusts, key considerations for administration, potential challenges, and best practices for ensuring their effectiveness. Whether managing a dynasty trust, an irrevocable asset protection trust, or a charitable remainder trust, trustees and beneficiaries must understand how these legal structures operate and how to optimize them.

TYPES OF COMPLEX TRUSTS

1. Irrevocable Trusts

Unlike revocable trusts, irrevocable trusts generally transfer assets out of the grantor's direct control. However, some irrevocable trusts are designed to allow the grantor to retain certain powers—particularly in grantor trusts—without undermining asset protection or tax planning.

Key Benefits:

• Estate tax reduction – When structured properly, assets may be removed from the grantor's taxable estate.

• Creditor and lawsuit protection – Assets can be shielded from legal judgments or claims.

• Medicaid and long-term care planning – Helps preserve assets for heirs while meeting eligibility rules (note: subject to the 5-year Medicaid lookback period).

• Income tax strategies – Particularly in intentionally defective grantor trusts (IDGTs), which allow income tax liability to remain with the grantor while transferring appreciation.

Challenges:

• May require court or beneficiary consent for modifications.

• Transfers must be made well in advance for Medicaid protection.

• Assets may still be taxed in the estate if retained powers are too extensive.

2. Dynasty Trusts

Dynasty trusts preserve wealth across multiple generations and can avoid estate taxation at each generational level when structured properly.

Key Benefits:

• Avoids generation-skipping transfer (GST) tax up to exemption amounts (currently $13.61 million per individual in 2024).

• Provides asset protection from divorce or lawsuits.

• Allows long-term growth outside the taxable estate.

Challenges:

• Must be designed to comply with state laws regarding perpetuity periods.

• Proper allocation of GST exemptions is essential.

• Requires long-term trustee management and strategic situs selection to minimize state income taxes.

3. Charitable Remainder Trusts (CRTs)

CRTs pay income to non-charitable beneficiaries for a period of time, with the remainder going to charity.

Key Benefits:

• Provides lifetime income.

• Immediate charitable income tax deduction.

• Reduces estate tax liability.

Challenges:

• Irrevocable structure limits access to funds.

• The charity must be qualified and named in the trust.

• Requires ongoing compliance with IRS rules.

4. Charitable Lead Trusts (CLTs)

The opposite of CRTs, CLTs pay income to charity for a specified term, with the remainder passing to heirs.

Key Benefits:

• Reduces taxable estate.

• Ideal for high-net-worth donors wanting to support charitable causes and pass wealth to family.

Challenges:

• Requires accurate valuation and risk management.

• Complex tax compliance.

5. Special Needs Trusts (SNTs)

SNTs support beneficiaries with disabilities without disqualifying them from public assistance.

Types:

• **First-party SNT** – Funded with the beneficiary's own assets and must include a Medicaid payback provision.

• **Third-party SNT** – Funded by others, does not require a payback provision.

Challenges:

• Must be carefully drafted to preserve benefit eligibility.

• Trustees must understand qualified distributions and reporting.

6. Grantor Retained Annuity Trusts (GRATs)

GRATs allow the grantor to transfer asset appreciation to heirs while retaining an annuity stream for a term.

Key Benefits:

• Efficient wealth transfer with little or no gift tax.

• Removes asset growth from taxable estate.

• Can be structured as a **"zeroed-out GRAT"** where the present value of the retained annuity equals the value of transferred assets, resulting in a near-zero taxable gift.

Challenges:

• Grantor must survive the annuity term.

• Complex valuation and risk management.

7. Intentionally Defective Grantor Trusts (IDGTs)

IDGTs freeze the value of an estate while shifting future appreciation to beneficiaries.

Key Benefits:

• Income tax is paid by the grantor, enhancing trust growth.

• Often used with promissory notes or sales of appreciating assets.

Challenges:

• Complex implementation.

• Requires coordination with estate planning and tax professionals.

8. Asset Protection Trusts (APTs)

Established in select jurisdictions or offshore, APTs shield assets from future creditors.

Types:

• **Domestic Asset Protection Trusts (DAPTs)** – Created in U.S. states like Nevada, Alaska, and Delaware.

• **Foreign Asset Protection Trusts (FAPTs)** – Set up in jurisdictions like the Cook Islands for stronger protection.

Key Benefits:

• Offers a high level of protection from lawsuits and claims.

• May allow the grantor to be a discretionary beneficiary.

Challenges:

• Must be created before creditor claims arise.

• Medicaid has a 5-year lookback period for transferred assets.

• Some states do not recognize DAPTs, and fraudulent conveyance laws must be respected.

9. Qualified Personal Residence Trusts (QPRTs)

QPRTs allow a grantor to transfer a personal residence or vacation home to heirs at a reduced gift tax cost.

Key Benefits:

• Removes future appreciation from taxable estate.

• Grantor can continue to live in the residence during the trust term.

Challenges:

• If the grantor dies during the term, the full value may be included in the estate.

• Limited flexibility once the property is in trust.

ADDITIONAL CONSIDERATIONS

Simple vs. Complex Trusts (for Income Tax Purposes)

• **Simple trusts** – Must distribute all income annually and cannot make charitable contributions.

• **Complex trusts** – Can retain income and make charitable donations. These are subject to more complex tax rules.

Trust Taxation

• Trusts reach the highest federal tax bracket (37%) at just $14,450 of income (2024).

• These thresholds are **adjusted annually for inflation**, so always check current IRS guidance.

• Strategic tax planning and selecting a low-tax situs state can reduce overall burdens.

Trust Situs and State Taxation

• State taxation varies widely; situs selection can affect tax liability, legal flexibility, and asset protection.

TOOLS FOR FLEXIBILITY AND ADAPTATION

• **Decanting** – Moving assets from one trust to another to revise terms.

• **Trust Protectors** – May amend terms, replace trustees, or clarify ambiguities.

- **Directed Trusts** – Allow different parties to handle administration, investments, and distribution decisions.
- **Silent Trusts** – Delay beneficiary disclosures to preserve family harmony.
- **Purpose Trusts** – Designed for non-charitable objectives like maintaining a pet or property.

TRUSTEE SELECTION CRITERIA

When selecting a trustee for a complex trust, consider:

- **Financial expertise** – Especially for investment-heavy trusts.
- **Legal understanding** – Ability to comply with fiduciary laws.
- **Neutrality** – Especially in families with potential conflict.
- **Capacity to administer across jurisdictions** – For trusts with real estate or foreign assets.

COMMON PITFALLS AND HOW TO AVOID THEM

1 **Failing to Monitor and Update the Trust** – Laws and family circumstances change.

2 **Improper Asset Titling** – Assets must be held in the trust to receive protection.

3 **Poor Trustee Selection** – Can lead to investment mismanagement or biased decision-making.

4 **Neglecting Legal Requirements** – Especially for modifying irrevocable trusts.

5 **Ignoring State Differences** – Situs laws can affect everything from duration to taxation.

6 Overlooking International Compliance – Failure to meet IRS rules for foreign trusts results in penalties.

7 Lack of Long-Term Planning – Dynasty trusts require coordinated tax and legal strategies.

CONCLUSION: ENSURING LONG-TERM SUCCESS FOR COMPLEX TRUSTS

Complex trusts provide significant advantages for estate planning, asset protection, and wealth transfer. However, their administration requires careful planning, professional guidance, and ongoing oversight. By understanding the different types of trusts, tax implications, and management responsibilities, trustees and beneficiaries can ensure that a complex trust fulfills its intended purpose for generations to come.

Key Takeaways:

- Complex trusts require advanced legal and tax structuring.
- Understand federal and state tax obligations, including income tax brackets and inflation adjustments.
- Always comply with international regulations and explore treaty benefits when applicable.
- Use tools like decanting and trust protectors to adapt to future needs.
- Choose qualified trustees based on competence and neutrality.
- Stay informed about emerging trust law developments.
- Work with qualified advisors to ensure ongoing success.

A well-structured trust, combined with proactive management and legal compliance, ensures that assets are preserved, beneficiaries are protected, and the grantor's legacy is upheld.

CHAPTER 16

PLANNING FOR INTERNATIONAL ASSETS AND FOREIGN BENEFICIARIES

INTERNATIONAL ASSETS AND FOREIGN HEIRS

As globalization increases, more U.S. citizens and permanent residents hold assets overseas or have heirs who live in or are citizens of other countries. Planning for these cross-border dynamics introduces additional layers of complexity to trust-based estate planning.

U.S. CITIZENS WITH FOREIGN PROPERTY

If you own real estate or financial accounts in another country, your U.S. trust may not automatically control those assets. Each country has its own legal system and property laws, and many do not recognize U.S.-based revocable living trusts.

Key challenges include:

• Foreign property may still be subject to that country's probate process, regardless of your U.S. trust

• Some countries have forced heirship laws, which override your estate planning intentions

• You may need to execute a will or trust compliant with the laws of that country to manage those assets effectively

Best practice: Work with an estate planning attorney familiar with international law and consider hiring local counsel in the country where the property is located. You may need to establish a separate foreign trust or will that coordinates with your U.S. plan.

REPORTING REQUIREMENTS: FATCA AND FBAR

U.S. citizens and residents must report foreign financial assets to the IRS under two primary rules:

• **FBAR (FinCEN Form 114):** Must be filed if you have foreign bank accounts totaling more than $10,000 at any time during the year

• **FATCA (Form 8938):** Requires reporting of foreign financial assets over certain thresholds (which vary based on filing status and residency)

Failing to meet these requirements can result in steep penalties. Trustees should be especially cautious when managing offshore accounts, foreign pensions, or investments held outside the U.S.

NON-U.S. CITIZEN SPOUSES AND HEIRS

Foreign Spouses

If your spouse is not a U.S. citizen, standard estate tax rules for married couples do not apply. While U.S. citizen spouses can inherit unlimited amounts tax-free, non-citizen spouses are subject to estate tax after a relatively low exemption amount.

Solution: Consider using a **Qualified Domestic Trust (QDOT)**, which allows you to defer estate taxes on assets left to a non-citizen spouse. The QDOT must meet specific IRS requirements and typically requires a U.S. trustee.

Foreign Heirs

When leaving assets to heirs who are not U.S. citizens or do not live in the U.S., consider:

- Whether the foreign country will impose inheritance taxes
- Currency conversion, local reporting, or restrictions on transfers
- Whether your trustee is permitted to transfer trust assets internationally

Also, keep in mind that U.S. gift and estate tax laws still apply to your estate, even when distributing assets abroad.

CONCLUSION

If your estate includes international property or heirs who live outside the U.S., you need to take extra care in structuring your trust and related documents. International coordination, tax reporting compliance, and planning for legal recognition across borders are essential to avoid unintended tax consequences or delays.

Cross-border estate planning requires legal professionals who understand the rules in both the U.S. and the relevant foreign jurisdictions. With proper planning, you can ensure your global estate is protected, compliant, and distributed as intended.

CHAPTER 17

COMMON TRUST DISPUTES AND HOW TO RESOLVE THEM

INTRODUCTION: UNDERSTANDING THE NATURE OF TRUST DISPUTES

Trusts are intended to facilitate smooth estate administration, protect assets, and ensure that a grantor's wishes are honored. However, despite careful planning, trust disputes can still arise due to miscommunication, unclear terms, conflicting beneficiary interests, or trustee mismanagement. These disputes can delay distributions, trigger costly legal battles, and, in extreme cases, even lead to the dissolution of the trust.

A well-structured trust should include clear instructions, defined trustee powers, and well-documented beneficiary rights to minimize conflicts. Even with these safeguards, disputes may emerge when interpretations of trust provisions differ, family tensions surface, or a trustee fails to uphold fiduciary duties. Fortunately, there are legal avenues available to resolve disputes through mediation, arbitration, or litigation if necessary.

This chapter examines the most common trust disputes, the legal grounds for contesting a trust, steps to resolve conflicts efficiently, and proactive measures to prevent disputes before they escalate.

WHY TRUST DISPUTES HAPPEN

1. Conflicts Among Beneficiaries

Trust disputes often stem from disagreements among beneficiaries. Whether due to family dynamics, perceived favoritism, or financial disputes, conflicts can intensify and hinder the administration process.

Common Causes:

- Unequal asset distribution
- Blended family dynamics
- Lack of transparency
- Delay in distributions
- Disagreements over sentimental assets

2. Allegations of Trustee Mismanagement

A trustee has a fiduciary duty to act in the best interests of the beneficiaries. When a trustee is perceived as acting negligently, dishonestly, or with favoritism, disputes arise.

Examples:

- Lack of communication
- Improper investments
- Self-dealing
- Failure to file tax returns
- Excessive trustee fees

- Conflict of interest
- Delays in distributions
- Failure to provide required accountings

3. Claims of Undue Influence or Lack of Capacity

A trust can be contested if a beneficiary or outside party believes that the grantor was manipulated into making certain provisions or lacked mental capacity.

Signs:

- Unusual last-minute changes
- Exclusion of long-standing heirs
- Isolation of the grantor
- Medical conditions like dementia
- Sudden new involvement in financial affairs
- Lack of proper documentation of mental capacity at time of signing

4. Ambiguous or Poorly Written Trust Terms

When trust provisions are unclear or contradictory, disputes are inevitable.

Examples:

- Vague language (e.g., "fair" distribution)
- No named successor trustee
- Conflicting instructions
- Discretionary distribution language without standards

5. Challenges to Trust Validity

Trusts can be contested if they were improperly created, executed, or contain fraudulent elements.

Legal Grounds:

- Failure to meet legal formalities
- Fraud or forgery
- Breach of fiduciary duty
- Coercion or duress
- Lack of capacity

Statute of Limitations:

- Varies by state; typically 120 days to 3 years after beneficiaries are notified of the trust.

Standing Requirements:

- Only interested parties (beneficiaries or those with a direct interest) may contest a trust.

Revocable vs. Irrevocable Trusts:

- Revocable trusts can usually be contested during the grantor's lifetime.
- Irrevocable trust contests often occur after the grantor's death and are subject to stricter timelines.

Jurisdictional Conflicts:

- Trusts with property in multiple states may require proceedings in more than one jurisdiction.

HOW TO AVOID TRUST DISPUTES

1. Clear and Precise Trust Drafting

• Use unambiguous language.

• Define distribution schedules and discretionary standards.

• Include a no-contest clause—while noting that many states will not enforce it if the contest is brought in good faith or with probable cause.

• Draft with the help of a qualified estate planning attorney.

2. Transparent Communication with Beneficiaries

• Hold periodic updates or meetings.

• Provide written financial statements.

• Document communication to prevent misunderstandings.

• Explain unequal distributions when appropriate.

3. Appointing the Right Trustee

• Consider a neutral party such as a corporate trustee.

• Choose someone organized, trustworthy, and impartial.

• Name successor trustees in case the primary trustee cannot serve.

• Consider a **trust protector** role to resolve future disagreements or replace trustees.

4. Using Alternative Dispute Resolution (ADR)

• **Mediation** – Informal, confidential, cost-effective resolution.

• **Arbitration** – Formal but private resolution with a binding outcome.

• **Non-judicial settlement agreements** – Allow parties to resolve certain disputes without court.

5. Legal Tools to Prevent Disputes

• Use **spendthrift provisions** to restrict beneficiary claims and creditor access.

• Consider **virtual representation**—where one beneficiary can represent the interests of others with similar rights.

• Leverage the **Uniform Trust Code (UTC)** where applicable, which outlines processes for trustee actions, trust modifications, and dispute resolution.

6. Protecting Vulnerable Beneficiaries

• Appoint a **guardian ad litem** for minors or incapacitated beneficiaries during legal disputes.

• Ensure proper documentation of the grantor's capacity—through capacity evaluations or videotaped signings.

CONCLUSION: RESOLVING AND PREVENTING TRUST DISPUTES

Trust disputes can damage family relationships, delay distributions, and result in substantial legal costs. However, proactive trust design, open communication, diligent trustee selection, and conflict resolution strategies can help prevent or resolve most issues.

Key Takeaways:

• Common disputes include beneficiary conflicts, ambiguous terms, trustee mismanagement, and undue influence.

• Contests require standing, timely filing, and must meet specific legal criteria.

- State-specific laws—including UTC adoption—impact how disputes are resolved.
- No-contest clauses are helpful but not always enforceable.
- Mediation, arbitration, and settlement agreements often resolve disputes faster and cheaper than litigation.
- Trust protectors, spendthrift clauses, and proper documentation reduce risk.
- A well-prepared trustee can prevent misunderstandings and build beneficiary trust.

By identifying and addressing potential conflict areas early, grantors and trustees can reduce the likelihood of disputes and protect the integrity of the estate plan.

CHAPTER 18
THE FUTURE OF LIVING TRUSTS

INTRODUCTION: HOW LIVING TRUSTS ARE EVOLVING

Estate planning is an ever-changing field shaped by technology, financial innovation, regulatory shifts, and changing family dynamics. Living trusts, once seen as static tools for probate avoidance, are now evolving rapidly to address emerging needs. From digital assets and artificial intelligence to blockchain, ESG investing, and global compliance issues, the landscape of trust planning is more dynamic than ever.

Grantors, trustees, and estate planning professionals must understand how these transformations will influence trust design, administration, and effectiveness. This chapter explores how these trends are changing the way trusts are created, managed, and adapted to meet the challenges of modern estate planning.

1. DIGITAL ASSETS AND THE RISE OF THE DIGITAL ESTATE

Cryptocurrency, NFTs, and Blockchain Assets

Living trusts are increasingly being used to manage nontraditional digital assets like cryptocurrencies and non-fungible tokens (NFTs). These types of assets present new estate planning challenges:

• **Private key security** – Loss of keys means total loss of the asset.

• **Fluctuating valuation** – Volatility complicates tax reporting.

• **Lack of centralized authority** – No institution can validate claims without prior planning.

Future-Focused Solutions:

• Multi-signature wallets to prevent unauthorized access.

• Smart contract-based inheritance mechanisms (where legally enforceable).

• Institutional-grade digital custody services.

• Legislative changes to clarify inheritance rights over digital assets.

Online Accounts, Intellectual Property, and Royalties

Trusts increasingly encompass:

• Social media accounts (via legacy tools).

• Online businesses and domain portfolios.

• Streaming royalties, e-book rights, and licensing revenues.

Estate planning must now include digital asset inventories and instructions for managing these rights.

2. THE ROLE OF ARTIFICIAL INTELLIGENCE IN TRUST MANAGEMENT

AI in Planning and Administration

AI is already enhancing estate planning:

• **Automated document drafting** with up-to-date compliance.

• **Financial forecasting** for trust growth and tax strategies.

• **Monitoring tools** that detect suspicious activity and mitigate risk.

AI as a Trustee? Legal Hurdles Remain

While the idea of AI-driven trustees is gaining attention, no current laws recognize artificial intelligence as having the legal capacity to act as a fiduciary. Still, hybrid models may emerge where human trustees leverage AI for:

• Optimized distribution timing.

• Dynamic rebalancing of trust portfolios.

• Compliance alerts.

3. BLOCKCHAIN AND SMART CONTRACTS IN ESTATE PLANNING

Blockchain has potential to transform trust infrastructure:

• **Smart contracts** can automate milestone-based distributions—though their enforceability varies by jurisdiction.

• **Tamper-proof ledgers** offer integrity for digital trust documents.

• **Global asset transfers** become more efficient through tokenization.

Estate planners must carefully integrate smart contracts into traditional legal structures to ensure enforceability.

4. LEGAL AND REGULATORY SHIFTS

Tax Reforms

• Rising exemption thresholds reduce the need for tax-focused trusts—but may reverse.

• Wealth tax proposals are increasing interest in dynasty and asset protection trusts.

• Capital gains tax changes could make step-up in basis planning more urgent.

Reporting and Compliance

• **FATCA** and **CRS** require financial institutions and trusts to report information about foreign accounts.

• Internationally administered trusts face greater transparency standards.

Remote Notarization and Electronic Signatures

• More states are adopting remote witnessing and e-signature laws.

• These developments simplify trust execution but raise new questions about document security.

5. EMERGING TRENDS IN TRUST STRUCTURES

Silent (or Quiet) Trusts

• Withhold information from beneficiaries until a triggering event.

• Useful in protecting minors or financially inexperienced heirs.

Directed Trusts

• Split responsibilities among investment advisors, distribution committees, and administrative trustees.

• Reduce liability and increase specialization.

Purpose Trusts

• Created for non-charitable objectives (e.g., care of pets, upkeep of property).

• Growing in popularity for long-term stewardship.

Hybrid Trusts

• Combine elements of revocable, irrevocable, domestic, and offshore trusts.

• Provide maximum adaptability.

Trust Protectors

• Individuals or institutions with the power to modify terms, replace trustees, or resolve disputes.

• Offer flexibility for long-term or multigenerational trusts.

Online Trust Platforms – Convenient, but Not One-Size-Fits-All

In recent years, several online platforms—such as **Trust & Will**, **LegalZoom**, and **Fabric**—have made estate planning more accessible and affordable. These services offer simplified tools to create basic wills and living trusts, often with guided forms and downloadable documents.

While these platforms can be helpful for individuals with **simple estates and straightforward goals**, they may not account for more complex issues such as:

- Blended families or strained family dynamics
- State-specific estate and tax laws
- Out-of-state real estate
- Special needs planning or asset protection
- Custom distribution terms or trustee provisions

Online tools should be seen as a **starting point**, not a substitute for legal advice. If your estate involves more than minimal assets or unique planning concerns, it's wise to review your documents with a qualified estate planning attorney to ensure they're valid, enforceable, and tailored to your situation.

6. ESG INVESTING AND TRUST ETHICS

Environmental, Social, and Governance (ESG) factors are playing a growing role in trust investment decisions:

- Beneficiaries increasingly request ethical or sustainable portfolios.
- Trustees must balance fiduciary duty with ethical investing mandates.
- New guidance may emerge to reconcile these goals within a prudent investor framework.

7. DEMOGRAPHIC AND SOCIAL SHIFTS

Aging Population

- Increased demand for successor trustee planning.
- Greater focus on long-term care directives and incapacity provisions.

Changing Family Structures

- More blended families, single-parent households, and unmarried partners.
- Trusts must address complex dynamics and clarify intent for each beneficiary class.

8. THE RISE OF BOUTIQUE AND ALTERNATIVE TRUST PROVIDERS

While traditional banks still dominate the trust industry, boutique and independent trust companies are gaining traction:

- Offer customized services with greater flexibility.
- Often more accessible and responsive than large institutions.
- Ideal for families with niche trust needs or global assets.

9. THE ROLE OF DECANTING IN FUTURE-PROOFING TRUSTS

Many states have passed decanting statutes, allowing trustees to move assets from an old trust into a new one with updated terms:

- Adapt to new laws or family situations.
- Add spendthrift or tax planning provisions.

- Modernize outdated language without court intervention.

10. PRIVACY AND DATA PROTECTION

As privacy laws like **GDPR** (Europe) and **CCPA** (California) expand, trustees must:

- Limit data sharing.
- Protect beneficiary information.
- Ensure compliance with cross-border data handling laws.

This is particularly crucial for trusts with international parties or online administration platforms.

CONCLUSION: ADAPTING TO THE FUTURE OF TRUSTS

Living trusts are no longer static legal tools—they are evolving financial frameworks. From digital asset management and blockchain to AI oversight and international compliance, the next generation of trusts will require agility, foresight, and collaboration between legal, financial, and technical professionals.

Key Takeaways:

- Digital assets and blockchain are reshaping estate planning strategies.
- AI and smart contracts offer innovation, but legal recognition remains a hurdle.
- ESG investing, demographic change, and global regulation are influencing trust structure.

• Trust administration is becoming more flexible through directed trusts, trust protectors, decanting, and silent trust provisions.

• Boutique firms are rising as alternatives to traditional trust institutions.

Staying informed about these developments is key to ensuring that living trusts remain secure, relevant, and effective in the decades to come.

CHAPTER 19

FINAL THOUGHTS AND BEST PRACTICES

INTRODUCTION: THE IMPORTANCE OF THOUGHTFUL TRUST PLANNING

Creating a living trust is one of the most effective ways to preserve wealth, minimize legal challenges, and ensure that assets are distributed according to a grantor's wishes. However, establishing a trust is only the first step—ongoing management, regular reviews, and clear communication with trustees and beneficiaries are essential to maintaining its effectiveness.

Estate planning is not a one-time event but a continuous process that requires periodic updates and adjustments. Life changes, shifts in financial circumstances, new privacy laws, evolving tax codes, and new technologies all necessitate a proactive approach to trust management. A well-maintained trust ensures financial stability for beneficiaries, reduces legal risks, and provides clear guidance for trustees.

This final chapter provides key takeaways, best practices, and actionable steps to help individuals, families, and trustees ensure their trust remains functional, compliant, and aligned with long-term goals.

KEY TAKEAWAYS FROM THIS BOOK

1 **Trusts provide flexibility and security** – A well-structured trust avoids probate, minimizes legal risk, and ensures that assets are distributed according to the grantor's intent.

2 **Regular updates are essential** – Trusts should be reviewed every three to five years and after major life events.

3 **Trustee selection is critical** – Appoint someone who is competent, ethical, and able to manage both finances and people.

4 **Tax efficiency must be considered** – Understanding estate, income, and capital gains taxes can help preserve the value of the estate.

5 **Clear communication prevents conflicts** – Transparency between grantors, trustees, and beneficiaries reduces the likelihood of disputes.

6 **Advanced planning accommodates complexity** – Living trusts can handle business succession, special needs, digital assets, and more.

7 **Proper funding is key** – A trust is only as effective as the assets it controls.

8 **Legal compliance is vital** – State and federal laws vary and evolve; ongoing legal review is essential.

9 **Digital assets must be addressed** – Cryptocurrency, online accounts, and intellectual property require specific planning.

10 Contingency planning ensures continuity – Design backup trustees, dispute resolution clauses, and long-term management strategies.

11 Document discretionary decisions – Trustees should document their reasoning for significant distributions or management choices.

12 Ethical wills or legacy letters add meaning – Including a personal letter or video message can preserve values and intentions alongside wealth.

BEST PRACTICES FOR EFFECTIVE TRUST MANAGEMENT

Regularly Review and Update the Trust

• Revisit your trust every 3–5 years or after any major life change.

• Restate the trust if there are multiple amendments or complex changes.

• Reevaluate successor trustees and confirm their willingness and ability to serve.

• Adjust the trust as necessary for new state-specific laws if you move between states.

• Ensure compliance with tax reform and estate planning best practices.

Ensure Proper Trust Funding

• Retitle real estate, investment accounts, and bank accounts to the trust.

• Link new assets to the trust as they are acquired.

• Use trust certification letters to facilitate transfers with financial institutions.

• Keep a detailed inventory of trust assets, including valuation data and account details.

• Reconfirm the trust owns any business interests or real property.

• Update retirement account and life insurance designations to align with trust strategy.

Choose the Right Trustee and Successor Trustee

• Select someone financially competent and emotionally impartial.

• Consider corporate or professional fiduciaries for complex or sensitive trusts.

• Define trustee powers and clearly outline responsibilities in writing.

• Provide ongoing education and encourage continuing legal or fiduciary training.

• Create a monitoring system or designate a trust protector to ensure accountability.

Keep Beneficiaries Informed

• Share the trust's purpose and structure with beneficiaries.

• Provide annual financial summaries and distribution schedules.

• Encourage open communication and address concerns early.

• Keep documentation of all communications and significant decisions.

• Offer beneficiaries financial literacy resources.

Stay Compliant with Tax Laws and Legal Requirements

• File IRS Form 1041 for applicable trusts and ensure proper reporting.

• Work with professionals to optimize income and estate tax outcomes.

• Maintain meticulous records for future audits or transitions.

• Stay informed on changing state and federal rules.

Plan for Digital Assets and Future Technologies

• Maintain an offline, secure record of private keys, passwords, and access protocols.

• Avoid storing sensitive information directly within the trust document.

• Use digital legacy tools (e.g., Apple Legacy Contact, Google Inactive Account Manager).

• Revisit your plan as digital technologies and asset classes evolve.

Incorporate Contingency Planning

• Define what happens if a trustee resigns, becomes incapacitated, or dies.

• Include dispute resolution clauses—mediation or arbitration—as alternatives to court.

• Specify final distribution plans and criteria for terminating the trust.

• Ensure liquidity or funding mechanisms are in place for emergencies.

• Plan for long-term care needs, incapacity, and unpredictable legal developments.

CONCLUSION: BUILDING A LASTING LEGACY

Trusts are more than legal tools—they are an opportunity to shape your financial legacy, safeguard your family's future, and reflect your personal values. Whether you're protecting your children, supporting a charitable mission, or managing complex investments, a proactive and well-managed trust can provide security and clarity for generations.

By applying the strategies and insights from this book, you can create a living trust that adapts to changing circumstances, remains legally sound, and fulfills your long-term vision. Most importantly, a living trust can be a vehicle for more than just wealth—it can pass along principles, stories, and stewardship that define your legacy.

WE'D LOVE YOUR FEEDBACK

If you found *Living Trusts Simplified* helpful, would you consider leaving a quick review?

Your feedback helps others find the book and allows us to continue creating accessible, practical estate planning guides.

You can leave a review here:

https://geni.us/LivingTrustsReview

Thank you for reading!

CHAPTER 20
NEXT STEPS TOOLKIT

ADDITIONAL RESOURCES & TOOLS

To assist you further in your estate planning journey, consider the following resources:

1. TRUST FUNDING CHECKLIST

• Ensure all titled assets (real estate, bank accounts, investments) are transferred into the trust.

• Confirm beneficiary designations for retirement accounts, insurance, and annuities.

• Address digital assets and out-of-state property appropriately.

• Store deeds, policies, and trust documents securely and accessibly.

2. QUESTIONS TO ASK AN ESTATE PLANNING ATTORNEY

- How do state laws affect my trust plan?
- What tax-saving strategies should I consider?
- How should I handle digital assets and online accounts?
- Do I need specialized trusts, such as special needs or asset protection trusts?

3. KEY IRS & GOVERNMENT RESOURCES

- IRS Estate and Gift Tax FAQs:

https://www.irs.gov/newsroom/estate-and-gift-tax-faqs

- IRS Estate Tax Information:

https://www.irs.gov/businesses/small-businesses-self-employed/estate-tax

- IRS Form 706 (Estate Tax Return):

https://www.irs.gov/forms-pubs/about-form-706

- State-by-State Estate Tax Information:

https://www.nolo.com/legal-encyclopedia/state-estate-taxes.html

4. DIGITAL ASSET PLANNING TOOLS

- Google Inactive Account Manager:

https://myaccount.google.com/inactive

- Facebook Legacy Contact Settings:

https://www.facebook.com/settings

• Consider using a password manager like 1Password, Dashlane, or LastPass for secure credential storage.

5. RECOMMENDED REVIEW SCHEDULE

• Every 2–3 years.

• After major life events (marriage, divorce, births, deaths, relocation).

• Following significant changes to tax laws or trust funding needs.

ACCESS YOUR LIVING TRUST COMPANION TOOLKIT

To help you take action on the strategies and information covered in this book, we've created a free downloadable Companion Toolkit. These resources are designed to simplify the trust creation and maintenance process and ensure your estate plan remains accurate and up to date.

You can download the full Toolkit here:

https://geni.us/LivingTrusts

WHAT'S INCLUDED IN THE TOOLKIT:

• **Trust Funding Checklist** - Step-by-step guide for properly transferring assets into your living trust.

• **Digital Asset Inventory Worksheet** - Record usernames, accounts, crypto keys, and cloud assets in one place.

• **Questions to Ask Your Estate Planning Attorney** - Bring these to your next consultation to get the most value from your meeting.

• **Beneficiary Review Log** - A tool to keep beneficiary designations consistent across your accounts and documents.

• **Annual Trust Review Template** - Helps you revisit and update your trust each year or after major life events.

• **Special Needs Planning Addendum** - For families caring for a beneficiary with disabilities or long-term needs.

HOW TO USE THE TOOLKIT:

• Review the Toolkit once a year, or whenever you experience a major life change (marriage, birth, relocation, etc.)

• Share completed documents with your successor trustee or attorney for safekeeping

• Keep digital copies in a secure password-protected location or vault

• Update information regularly and record any changes in your trust file

Reminder: These tools are meant to support—not replace—professional legal guidance. Always review major decisions or documents with an estate planning attorney licensed in your state.

You can download the complete toolkit for free at:

https://geni.us/LivingTrusts

(Or scan the QR code below with your phone or tablet)

Why Use It?

These resources make it easier to work with your attorney, stay organized, and ensure your trust continues to reflect your wishes as life changes.

https://geni.us/LivingTrusts

Pro Tip: Share relevant documents with your successor trustee so they understand what to expect and where to find key information.

Note: Always review completed forms with your estate planning attorney before relying on them for legal or tax purposes.

CHAPTER 21

BONUS CHAPTER: WHEN TO DIY AND WHEN TO CALL A LAWYER

WHEN TO DIY AND WHEN TO CALL A LAWYER

Creating a living trust is one of the most valuable steps you can take to protect your assets and your family—but knowing how much of it you can do on your own versus when to seek professional help is just as important. While online tools and templates have made trust creation more accessible, there are still many scenarios where hiring an estate planning attorney is not only wise but essential.

This bonus chapter will help you understand where the DIY route is sufficient, and where legal expertise is necessary to avoid costly mistakes.

WHEN A DIY APPROACH MAY BE SUFFICIENT

If your situation is relatively straightforward, you may be able to create and fund a basic revocable living trust using an online service or software, especially if you:

- Are single or part of a married couple with similar goals

- Have adult children and no minor dependents
- Own a single home and a few financial accounts
- Do not own property in multiple states or countries
- Have a clear and uncontested plan for who inherits what
- Are not concerned about asset protection, Medicaid eligibility, or estate taxes

In these situations, services like LegalZoom, Trust & Will, or other attorney-reviewed document platforms may offer enough guidance to complete a basic trust—provided you're comfortable following instructions and doing some due diligence.

Important: Even if you go the DIY route, consider having your documents reviewed by a professional. A 1–2 hour consultation can offer peace of mind.

WHEN YOU SHOULD ABSOLUTELY WORK WITH AN ATTORNEY

More complex situations require expert legal guidance. You should consult with a qualified estate planning attorney if:

- You have a blended family, stepchildren, or estranged heirs
- You have minor children or are setting up a guardian structure
- You own a business, rental property, or assets in multiple states or countries
- You or your spouse are not U.S. citizens
- You want to include asset protection provisions or irrevocable trusts
- You plan to leave money to a beneficiary with special needs

- You want to minimize estate taxes or set up charitable giving strategies
- You're concerned about family conflict or want to include no-contest clauses
- You need help coordinating retirement account beneficiaries or complex tax planning

In these situations, an attorney can help you structure your trust correctly, avoid unintended legal consequences, and create custom provisions to match your specific goals.

RED FLAGS FOR DIY TRUSTS

Even simple situations can become complex quickly. Watch out for these common red flags:

- You don't understand what "funding the trust" means
- You're not sure how to retitle real estate or financial accounts
- You have questions about what to leave in the trust vs. out
- You're unsure whether your trust works with your will, power of attorney, or medical directives
- You're not confident the documents are valid in your state

If you're hitting any of these walls, it's a strong sign you should bring in professional help.

A HYBRID APPROACH THAT WORKS

Many people successfully use a "hybrid" method:

1 **Start with a DIY draft** to clarify your wishes and organize your assets

2 Meet with an attorney to review, customize, and ensure state compliance

3 Use the Toolkit (Chapter 20) to stay organized and keep documents updated

This method can save money while still ensuring legal accuracy and peace of mind.

CONCLUSION

Your living trust is a powerful tool—but only if it's done correctly. For some, an online service may be enough. For others, legal counsel is essential. When in doubt, spend the time (and the modest investment) to make sure it's done right. The cost of errors—missed assets, probate, family conflict—can far outweigh the upfront savings.

Remember: A good estate plan isn't just about documents. It's about clarity, control, and confidence for you and your loved ones.

CHAPTER 22

BONUS CHAPTER: PLANNING ACROSS STATE LINES

PLANNING ACROSS STATE LINES

Estate planning is governed primarily by state law, and while many principles are similar across the U.S., key details—such as probate procedures, community property rules, and trust formalities—can vary significantly from one state to another. If you move, own property in multiple states, or live in a community property state, it's critical to understand how your trust interacts with local laws.

This bonus chapter will help you anticipate and navigate state-specific considerations.

WHAT DOESN'T CHANGE

The good news is that most properly written revocable living trusts remain valid even if you move to another state. If your trust was created according to the laws of your previous state and you followed appropriate formalities (witnessing, notarization, etc.), it will still be recognized in your new state.

However, there are areas where laws differ—and ignoring them can create unintended consequences.

WHAT MAY CHANGE BASED ON YOUR STATE

1. Probate Rules and Exemptions

Each state has its own threshold for when probate is required. Some states allow streamlined processes for small estates, while others are more rigid.

• Example: In California, probate can be required for estates over $184,500 (as of 2023), whereas in Arizona it may start at $75,000.

If your trust isn't fully funded or updated after a move, your estate could be subject to probate in your new state.

2. Community Property vs. Common Law States

If you live in a **community property state** (AZ, CA, ID, LA, NV, NM, TX, WA, WI), different rules apply to how marital assets are owned and passed along.

• In these states, assets acquired during marriage are typically owned 50/50 by both spouses, regardless of title.

• A trust can still be used, but it should reflect community property treatment to ensure step-up in basis and proper control.

If you move from a common law state to a community property state (or vice versa), revisit your trust and how assets are titled.

3. Real Estate in Multiple States

If you own homes or land in more than one state, you could face **ancillary probate** if those properties aren't included in your trust.

- Be sure to execute **state-specific deeds** transferring each property into the trust.
- Use an estate planning attorney familiar with real estate laws in each state involved.

4. Powers of Attorney and Advance Directives

While trusts tend to be portable, **POAs and healthcare directives** are more sensitive to state formats.

- Some medical providers may not honor an out-of-state directive.
- Re-signing these documents when you move is a smart precaution.

HOW TO STAY COMPLIANT WHEN MOVING

- **Review your trust documents with an attorney licensed in your new state**
- **Update deeds** for real estate as required by local recording offices
- **Re-sign powers of attorney and healthcare directives** using state-specific forms
- **Check titling and beneficiary designations** for consistency
- **Understand your state's probate and tax laws**—some states have inheritance or estate taxes that others do not

WHERE TO FIND STATE-SPECIFIC INFORMATION

You don't have to become an expert in local trust law—but knowing where to look can make a big difference:

- Visit your **state's bar association** website and search for estate planning or elder law sections
- Look up your **county probate court** for local filing thresholds and small estate procedures
- Use resources like **Nolo.com**, **LawHelp.org**, or **your local AARP office** for consumer-friendly legal guidance
- Ask your estate planning attorney if they are part of a **national network** and can refer you to colleagues in other states

CONCLUSION

Moving to a new state or owning property across state lines doesn't invalidate your trust—but it does mean it's time for a checkup. A small investment in reviewing your documents and updating local filings can prevent future probate, tax issues, or confusion for your heirs. Trusts are powerful, but they must be maintained properly within each state's legal framework.

CHAPTER 23

BONUS CHAPTER: SPECIAL CASES AND SCENARIOS

SPECIAL CASES AND SCENARIOS

Living trusts are highly flexible tools, but certain life situations call for extra attention. This chapter highlights specific scenarios where careful planning or customized provisions can make the difference between a smooth estate transition and a legal or financial mess.

SINGLE INDIVIDUALS WITH NO CHILDREN

Many people assume living trusts are only for families or high-net-worth individuals. Not true. A trust can:

• Ensure your assets go to your chosen friends, relatives, or charities

• Avoid the need for court-appointed conservatorship if you become incapacitated

• Help avoid probate, even with a small estate

Tips:

• Choose a trusted friend or professional as your successor trustee

• Use the trust to make gifts to organizations or causes you care about

DIGITAL-ONLY OR PAPERLESS ESTATES

If most of your assets are online—like investment apps, crypto, or stored in the cloud—a traditional estate plan may fall short.

• Be sure to inventory digital accounts and provide access instructions

• Use a **Digital Asset Inventory Worksheet** (see Toolkit)

• Choose a trustee comfortable with tech or digital records

FREQUENT MOVERS OR INTERNATIONAL TRAVEL

If you change your state of residence regularly or spend large parts of the year abroad:

• Make sure your trust is reviewed in each new state (see Bonus Chapter B)

• Include backup communication methods for your trustee

• Store documents securely online and share access credentials with your trustee

MULTILINGUAL OR CROSS-CULTURAL FAMILIES

If your heirs speak multiple languages or live in different countries, add:

• Plain-language summaries of your trust

- Clear contact info for your attorney or trustee
- Multilingual guidance (if appropriate)

FINANCIALLY INEXPERIENCED HEIRS

If your heirs are not yet ready to manage money responsibly, consider:

- Staggered distributions (e.g., 25% at age 25, 50% at 30, remainder at 35)
- Trustee discretion to delay or deny payouts in cases of addiction, debt, or instability
- Including educational incentives or achievement triggers

BUSINESS OWNERS

If you own a business (LLC, S-Corp, or sole proprietorship):

- Include the business interest in your trust
- Update your operating agreement or shareholder agreement to reflect your trust
- Appoint a trustee who understands the business—or name a separate business manager

PETS OR NON-HUMAN BENEFICIARIES

Yes, you can create a pet trust!

- Set aside funds for the care of a pet
- Name a caregiver and a trustee to oversee the funds
- Specify care instructions, veterinary preferences, and remainder beneficiaries if the pet dies

OTHER SPECIAL SITUATIONS WORTH PLANNING FOR

Every family is different, and there are additional scenarios where special planning can help protect your assets and reduce the risk of conflict:

Disinheriting an Heir

If you plan to disinherit a child or relative, it's important to be explicit in your trust. Simply omitting someone's name may create legal ambiguity. Consider:

- Including a clear statement of intent (e.g., "I am intentionally not providing for [Name]")
- Using a **no-contest clause** to discourage legal challenges
- Consulting an attorney to ensure the language is enforceable under your state's laws

Beneficiaries with Addiction or Behavioral Challenges

If an heir struggles with substance abuse, gambling, or other high-risk behavior:

- Use a **discretionary trust** with a trustee who can restrict or delay distributions
- Allow funds to be used for rehab, housing, or health care, but not cash disbursements
- Include behavioral or milestone-based triggers for future distributions

Shielding Assets in Divorce

While revocable trusts don't offer divorce protection during your lifetime, they can:

- Protect your children's inheritance from being commingled in their future marriages
- Allow you to control whether a child's spouse has access to trust funds
- Be combined with **spendthrift** or **asset protection trust** provisions in irrevocable structures

CONCLUSION

Living trusts are not one-size-fits-all. Your life is unique—and your estate plan should be too. These special scenarios remind us that a well-designed trust isn't just about avoiding probate; it's about protecting what matters, in the way that matters most to you. If any of these apply, work with your attorney to tailor your trust accordingly.

CHAPTER 24

BONUS CHAPTER: USEFUL TOOLS & SERVICES FOR ESTATE PLANNING

USEFUL TOOLS & SERVICES FOR ESTATE PLANNING

Estate planning today is easier than ever thanks to a growing number of digital tools, online services, and secure platforms that simplify document creation, organization, and long-term administration. Whether you're creating your own trust, managing a loved one's estate, or just staying organized, the right tools can make a big difference.

This chapter offers a curated list of helpful resources for different parts of the estate planning process.

1. ONLINE TRUST CREATION PLATFORMS

These tools help individuals create revocable living trusts, wills, powers of attorney, and healthcare directives with step-by-step guidance.

- **Trust & Will** – Clean interface, attorney-reviewed documents, good customer support

• **LegalZoom** – Long-standing service with broad legal document support

• **Fabric by Gerber Life** – Offers free will creation and simple estate tools

• **FreeWill** – Easy-to-use, donation-driven platform for basic estate planning documents

Note: While these services can be helpful for simple estates, they may not replace an experienced attorney—especially for complex situations.

2. TRUST ADMINISTRATION SOFTWARE (FOR TRUSTEES & PROFESSIONALS)

These platforms help manage trust distributions, reporting, asset tracking, and communication among beneficiaries.

• **Estateably** – Cloud-based platform designed for professionals administering trusts and estates

• **Wealth.com** – Personal estate planning and tracking platform for modern families

• **TrustBooks** – For small law firms and professional fiduciaries who manage trusts

3. PASSWORD MANAGERS & DIGITAL VAULTS

Use these tools to securely store digital account logins, important documents, and access information for your trustee.

• **1Password** – User-friendly and highly secure password manager

• **Dashlane** – Includes secure file storage and dark web monitoring

- **LastPass** – Strong free tier and family plans for shared access
- **Everplans** – End-of-life planning tool that stores wills, insurance, and other legacy documents securely

4. DOCUMENT STORAGE & SHARING

Keep your trust, will, power of attorney, and related forms organized and accessible.

- **Dropbox** or **Google Drive** – Familiar, cloud-based storage for digital copies (use strong permissions)
- **DocuBank** – Medical directive registry with 24/7 access for hospitals and doctors
- **LifeSite** – Secure family dashboard to manage legal, financial, and healthcare documents

5. STATE-SPECIFIC RESOURCES

Each state has its own legal requirements, forms, and probate rules. Use these links to explore:

- Your **state bar association** (search "estate planning section")
- Your **county probate court** for local filing thresholds
- **LawHelp.org** or **Nolo.com** for consumer legal guides
- Local **AARP offices** for state-by-state senior planning guides

6. FINDING AN ESTATE PLANNING ATTORNEY

- **NAELA.org** – National Academy of Elder Law Attorneys
- **ACTEC.org** – American College of Trust and Estate Counsel

- **Avvo.com** – Search for rated estate planning attorneys in your area
- Ask your financial advisor, CPA, or insurance agent for a trusted referral

CONCLUSION

While a living trust is a legal document, it's also a living system —one that needs to be created, maintained, and revisited as life changes. With the right mix of tools, platforms, and professional support, you can ensure your plan remains secure, accessible, and aligned with your wishes. Use these resources to stay organized, protect your assets, and simplify the trust management process for your loved ones.

FREQUENTLY ASKED QUESTIONS ABOUT LIVING TRUSTS

1. Do I need a living trust if I already have a will?

Yes. A will only goes into effect after death and requires probate. A living trust helps you manage your assets during life and ensures a smooth transfer upon death—without court involvement.

2. Can I be my own trustee?

Yes. Most people name themselves as the initial trustee and retain full control during their lifetime. You will also name a successor trustee to manage the trust if you become incapacitated or pass away.

3. What happens if I forget to transfer an asset into my trust?

If you have a pour-over will, it can catch forgotten assets and transfer them into your trust after death—though they may still go through probate. Regular reviews and funding checklists help prevent this.

4. Can a living trust protect my assets from creditors or lawsuits?

A **revocable** trust does not offer asset protection, since you still control the assets. However, **irrevocable** trusts can offer protection if structured properly and established before any claims arise.

5. Do I lose control of my assets if I put them in a living trust?

No. With a revocable trust, you can still buy, sell, manage, or remove assets as you wish. The trust is fully under your control while you're alive and competent.

6. Can a trust own my retirement accounts (IRA, 401k)?

No. Retirement accounts should not be retitled in the name of the trust. Instead, your trust can be named as a **beneficiary**, if properly structured to avoid tax complications.

7. Will creating a trust avoid all taxes?

No. A living trust helps with efficient estate transfer and may support tax strategies, but it doesn't automatically eliminate estate, gift, or income taxes. Strategic planning is required.

8. How often should I update my trust?

Review your trust every 3–5 years or after major life events such as marriage, divorce, births, deaths, relocation, or significant changes in tax laws.

9. Can I make changes to my trust?

If it's **revocable**, yes—you can amend or restate the trust at any time. If it's **irrevocable**, changes are limited and often require beneficiary or court approval.

10. Do I need an attorney to create a trust?

Technically, no—but using an experienced estate planning attorney is highly recommended to ensure your trust is legally valid, properly funded, and tailored to your needs.

GLOSSARY OF COMMON ESTATE PLANNING TERMS

Administrator – A person appointed by the court to manage an estate when there is no will or named executor.

Advance Directive – A legal document that outlines a person's preferences for medical treatment if they become incapacitated. Includes living wills and healthcare proxies.

Asset – Any item of value owned by an individual, such as real estate, bank accounts, investments, vehicles, or personal property.

Beneficiary – A person or organization named to receive assets from a will, trust, retirement account, or life insurance policy.

Capital Gains Tax – A tax on the profit from the sale of an asset. Inherited assets typically receive a step-up in basis, reducing capital gains tax.

Decedent – A person who has passed away.

Estate – The total sum of a person's assets, liabilities, and possessions at the time of their death.

Estate Tax – A tax levied on the estate of a deceased person before distribution to heirs. Applies only to estates above certain thresholds.

Executor – The person named in a will to carry out the terms of the will and manage the estate through probate.

Fiduciary – A person who has the legal and ethical duty to act in the best interest of another. Trustees, executors, and agents under a power of attorney are all fiduciaries.

Funding a Trust – The act of transferring assets into a trust so they are governed by the terms of the trust.

Grantor – The person who creates and funds the trust. Also called a settlor or trustor.

Healthcare Proxy – A person authorized to make medical decisions on behalf of someone who is incapacitated. Also known as a healthcare agent.

Irrevocable Trust – A trust that cannot be changed or revoked after it is established, except in limited circumstances. Used for asset protection and tax planning.

Living Will – A document that outlines an individual's wishes for medical treatment in the event of a terminal illness or permanent unconsciousness.

Pour-Over Will – A simple will used in conjunction with a trust. It directs any assets not already in the trust to be transferred to the trust after death.

Power of Attorney (POA) – A legal document that allows a person (the agent) to act on behalf of another (the principal) in financial or legal matters.

Probate – The court-supervised process of settling an estate, including validating a will, paying debts, and distributing assets.

Revocable Trust – A trust that can be amended or revoked at any time by the grantor during their lifetime.

Successor Trustee – A person or institution appointed to take over management of a trust after the original trustee dies or becomes incapacitated.

Testator – A person who creates a will.

Trust – A legal arrangement in which a grantor places assets under the management of a trustee for the benefit of one or more beneficiaries.

Trustee – The individual or institution responsible for managing trust assets and following the trust's terms.

Will – A legal document that outlines how a person's assets should be distributed after death. Wills must go through probate.

Made in the USA
Monee, IL
13 September 2026

62976608R00098